the Pomodoro Technique

the Pomodoro Technique

THE ACCLAIMED TIME-MANAGEMENT SYSTEM
THAT HAS TRANSFORMED HOW WE WORK

Francesco Cirillo

CURRENCY
NEW YORK

Copyright © 2006, 2018 by Francesco Cirillo

All rights reserved.
Published in the United States by Currency,
an imprint of the Crown Publishing Group,
a division of Penguin Random House LLC, New York.
crownpublishing.com

CURRENCY and its colophon are trademarks of Penguin Random House LLC.

Originally self-published in a different form as *The Pomodoro Technique: Do More and Have Fun with Time Management* in 2006.

Currency books are available at special discounts for bulk purchases for sales promotions or corporate use. Special editions, including personalized covers, excerpts of existing books, or books with corporate logos, can be created in large quantities for special needs. For more information, contact Premium Sales at (212) 572-2232 or e-mail specialmarkets@penguinrandomhouse.com.

Library of Congress Cataloging-in-Publication Data is available upon request.

ISBN 978-1-5247-6070-0
Ebook ISBN 978-1-5247-6071-7

PRINTED IN THE UNITED STATES OF AMERICA

Book design by Andrea Lau
Jacket design by Christopher Lin
Jacket photograph: PackStock/Alamy Stock Photo

10 9 8 7 6 5 4 3 2 1

2018 Currency Edition

CONTENTS

REACHING YOUR TEAM GOALS

RESULTS

PREFACE TO THE 2018 EDITION

I WOUND UP the first Pomodoro on a cloudy September afternoon in 1987. The setting was the terrace of a house in a medieval village 30 miles north of Rome—Sutri—where I spent my family holidays. The task was clear but scary: "I want to finish this chapter." The chapter in question was the first of the sociology book I was reading for a university exam I had to take within a few weeks.

That afternoon, I never imagined that one day millions of people around the world would have repeated that same gesture of winding up a kitchen timer to beat distractions and reach their objectives within the set period of time. I never imagined that I would hear the sound of ticking timers in the background upon entering an open-space office full of brilliant software developers. And I would have thought it impossible for the CEO of a bank to use my same tomato-shaped timer to structure a board meeting. Or that the technique would be described in such prestigious publications as the *New York Times*, *The Guardian*, and *Harvard Business Review*. Yet, all that did happen. But how it happened still remains a pleasant mystery to me.

I clearly remember the sensation I felt when that Pomodoro rang for the first time: an unusual and unexplainable sense of calm. My mind had been drifting from one direction to another like a small boat at the mercy of a storm. "I need to pass the exam. I have three books to study. There's not much time until the exam. I'll never make it. I can't focus. I'm always getting distracted. Maybe I should stop studying and postpone the exam. Maybe I should stop studying and do something else." After the Pomodoro rang, and that first timed work period was over, the sea was calm again: I knew I could do it. I remember wanting to set another Pomodoro. And I had set that first one for only two minutes, not the 25 I would come to find was ideal.

It was that sense of calmness and control I had regained that enabled me to pass the exam. And led me to start my own research into the phenomenon of Pomodoros: "Why does it work? How long should a Pomodoro last? How many Pomodoros can you do in a day? How much rest between Pomodoros should I allow?" It took a number of years to find the answers to those questions and to organize and structure them into a technique for improving productivity. I felt it was natural to name the technique I had developed the Pomodoro.

As I write this preface, the gentle ticking of that Pomodoro kitchen timer I used to prepare for the sociology exam is still with me. It has become an old friend. Thirty-one years have passed since that September afternoon in 1987. Many things have changed since then. The development of the Internet and social media have transformed our habits and behavior. Our smartphones let us know when we need to leave to get to the movies on time or when the dinner we ordered from the car or taxi on the way home is five minutes away from being delivered. Social media and various apps expose us to interruptions 24/7. So how is the Pomodoro Technique still effective in the digital age?

The most prolific source of distractions remains our own mind. What I call internal interruptions—the sudden desire to order a pizza, update your social media status, or clean your desk—can still be more frequent and disruptive than the external ones, such as the ping of a new e-mail or a Facebook notification. The best approach to dealing with these interruptions is to accept them and **treat them in a gentle way.** The Pomodoro Technique invites you to write them down on your phone or computer or a piece of paper and deal with them once your Pomodoro is over. This way, you acknowledge their value and have time to consider and assess them properly to decide whether they are really important or not. If in a short space of time you experience too many internal interruptions, the Pomodoro Technique specifically requires you to stop and take a longer break.

The appearance of so many internal interruptions is our mind's way of sending us a message: We are not at ease with what we are doing. This may be because the prospect of failing worries us—it can be scary. Or maybe our goal seems too complex or we feel we are running out of time. To protect us, our minds come up with different, more reassuring activities. We end up favoring interruptions wherever we can latch on to them.

The type and frequency of interruptions—whether they are internal or external—do not threaten the Pomodoro Technique. The technique helps us be aware of how our mind works and helps us to consciously decide how to deal with interruptions. Sometimes what pops into our head is truly urgent. But in most cases, it can be postponed for 20 minutes, until the end of the Pomodoro. Because interruptions are often just ways for our mind to distract us, taking us away from what we are supposed to be doing, this process can lead you to a better understanding of the fears that underlie your reaction to interruptions. Once you identify these fears, you can find ways to manage them. Without this process, our fears can take over and a "fear of fear" can paralyze us. The technique helps us develop a constant dialogue with ourselves, to observe ourselves and not delude ourselves. In any case, if you find yourself writing messages instead of focusing on your goal, do not worry: **The next Pomodoro will go better.** Be gentle with yourself.

PREFACE

THE BASIC IDEA for the Pomodoro Technique came to me in the late 1980s, during my first years at college.

Once the elation from completing my first-year examinations had subsided, I found myself in a slump, a time of low productivity and high confusion. Every day I went to school, attended classes, and returned home with the disheartening feeling that I didn't know what I'd been doing, that I'd been wasting my time. The exam dates came up so fast, and it seemed that I had no way to defend myself against the passing of time.

One day in the classroom on campus where I used to study, I watched my classmates with a critical eye and then looked even more critically at myself: how I got myself organized, how I interacted with others, how I studied. It was clear that the high number of distractions and interruptions and the low level of concentration and motivation were at the root of the confusion I was feeling.

I asked myself a question that was as helpful as it was humiliating: "Can you study—really study—for ten minutes?" I needed objective validation, a Time Tutor, and I found one in a kitchen timer shaped like a *pomodoro* (Italian for tomato)—in other words, I found my Pomodoro.

I didn't win the bet I made with myself about studying right away. In fact, it took time and a great deal of effort, but in the end I succeeded.

In that first small step, I found something intriguing in the Pomodoro mechanism. With this new tool, I devoted myself to improving my study process and later my work process. I tried to understand and solve more and more complex problems, to the point of considering the dynamics of teamwork. Gradually I put together the Pomodoro Technique, which I describe in this book.

For years I've taught the Pomodoro Technique in classes open to the public and in team mentoring. In that time, general interest has grown. More and more people are asking what it is and how to apply it, and so there's a need for me to explain the technique as I conceived it. My hope is that it can help others reach their goals for personal improvement.

INTRODUCTION

OR MANY PEOPLE, time is an enemy. The anxiety triggered by the ticking clock, particularly when a deadline is involved, leads to ineffective work and study behavior, which in turn elicits the tendency to procrastinate. The Pomodoro Technique was created with the aim of using time as a valuable ally to accomplish what we want to do the way we want to do it and to empower us to improve our work or study progress continuously. This book presents the Pomodoro Technique as it was developed in 1992 and as it has been taught to individuals since 1998 and to teams since 1999.

The Foundations section delineates the problem linked to time and the goals of the Pomodoro Technique and its basic assumptions. The Reaching Your Individual Goals section describes the Pomodoro Technique and shows how individuals can apply it by completing incremental objectives. The Reaching Your Team Goals section explains how to adapt the technique to a team and describes a series of practices to improve a team's productivity. The Results section provides a series of observations that are based on the experiences of people who have used the technique and identifies a number of factors that explain how the technique achieves its goals.

FOUNDATIONS

THE CONTEXT

WHO HASN'T EXPERIENCED anxiety when faced with a task that has to be finished by a deadline? In these circumstances, who hasn't felt the need to put off that task or fallen behind schedule or procrastinated? Who hasn't had that unpleasant sensation of depending on time, chasing after appointments, giving up what one loves to do for lack of time?

"Remember, Time is a greedy player who wins without cheating, every round!" Baudelaire wrote in his poem "The Clock." Is this the true nature of time? Or is it only one of the possible ways to consider time? More generally, why do people have such a problem in the way they relate to time? Where does it come from, this anxiety that we've all experienced at the thought that time is slipping away?

Thinkers, philosophers, scientists—anyone who's taken on the challenge of attempting to define time and the relationship between people and time—always have been forced to admit defeat. Such an inquiry, in fact, is inevitably limited and never complete. Few have provided any truly insightful perspectives. Two profoundly interrelated aspects seem to coexist in regard to time:

- **BECOMING.** An abstract, dimensional aspect of time that gives rise to the habit of measuring time (seconds, minutes, hours); the idea of representing time on an axis, as we would spatial dimensions; the concept of the duration of an event (the distance between two points on the temporal axis); the idea of being late (again the distance between two points on the temporal axis).[1]

- **THE SUCCESSION OF EVENTS.** A concrete aspect of temporal order: We wake up, we shower, we have breakfast, we study, we have lunch, we have a nap, we play, we eat, and we go to bed. Children come to have this notion of time before they develop the idea of abstract time that passes regardless of the events that take place.[2]

Of these two aspects, it is *becoming* that generates anxiety. It is by nature elusive, indefinite, infinite: Time passes, slips away, moves toward the future. If we try to measure ourselves against the passage of time, we feel inadequate, oppressed, enslaved, and defeated more and more with every second that goes by. We lose our élan vital, the life force that enables us to accomplish things: "Two hours have gone by and I'm still not done; two days have gone by and I'm still not done." In moments of weakness, the purpose of the activity at hand is no longer clear. The succession of events seems to be the less anxiety-ridden aspect of time. At

---

[1]   Henri Bergson, *Creative Evolution*, Book Jungle, 2009.

[2]   Eugène Minkowski, *Lived Time*, Northwestern University Press, 1970.

times it may even represent the regular succession of activity, a calm-inducing rhythm.

GOALS OF THE POMODORO TECHNIQUE

The aim of the Pomodoro Technique is to provide a simple tool/ process for improving productivity (your own and that of your team). It can do the following:

- Alleviate anxiety linked to *becoming*
- Enhance focus and concentration by cutting down on interruptions
- Increase awareness of one's decisions
- Boost motivation and keep it constant
- Bolster the determination to achieve one's goals
- Refine the estimation process in both qualitative and quantitative terms
- Improve one's work or study process
- Strengthen one's determination to keep applying oneself in complex situations

BASIC ASSUMPTIONS

The Pomodoro Technique is founded on three key elements:

- **A DIFFERENT WAY OF SEEING TIME** that no longer is focused on the concept of *becoming*. This alleviates anxiety and thus leads to enhanced personal effectiveness.
- **BETTER USE OF THE MIND.** This enables us to achieve greater clarity of thought, higher consciousness, and sharper focus while facilitating learning.

- **THE EMPLOYMENT OF EASY-TO-USE, UNOBTRUSIVE TOOLS.** This reduces the complexity of applying the technique while favoring continuity and allows us to concentrate our efforts on the goals we want to accomplish. Many time-management techniques fail because they add another level of complexity to the intrinsic complexity of the task at hand.

The primary inspiration for the Pomodoro Technique came from the following ideas: time-boxing; the cognitive techniques described by Buzan,[3] among others, relating to the way the mind works; and the dynamics of play outlined by Gadamer.[4] Notions relating to structuring objectives and activities incrementally are detailed in Gilb.[5]

---

[3]   Tony Buzan, *The Brain User's Guide*, Plume, 1983.

[4]   Hans-Georg Gadamer, *Truth and Method*, Continuum, 2004.

[5]   Tom Gilb, *Principles of Software Engineering Management*, Addison-Wesley, 1996.

REACHING YOUR
INDIVIDUAL GOALS

·|·|·|·|·|·|·|·|·|·|·|·

MATERIAL AND METHOD

THE PROCESS UNDERLYING the Pomodoro Technique consists of five stages:

WHAT	WHEN	WHY
Planning	At the start of the day	To decide on the day's activities
Tracking	Throughout the day	To gather raw data on the effort expended and other metrics of interest
Recording	At the end of the day	To compile an archive of daily observations
Processing	At the end of the day	To transform raw data into information
Visualizing	At the end of the day	To present the information in a format that facilitates understanding and clarifies paths to improvement

TABLE 1: THE STAGES OF THE POMODORO TECHNIQUE

☞ This basic procedure lasts one day but could take less time. In that case, the five stages would take place more frequently.

FIGURE 1: THE POMODORO

To implement the Pomodoro Technique, all you need is the following:

- A Pomodoro: a kitchen timer (Figure 1).
- A *To Do Today Sheet* filled in at the start of each day with the following:
  - A heading with place, date, and author.
  - A list of the things to do during the day in order of priority.
  - A section labeled "Unplanned & Urgent Activities" in which any unexpected tasks that have to be dealt with should be listed as they come up. These activities could modify the day's plan.
- An *Activity Inventory Sheet* consisting of the following:
  - A heading with the name of the author.
  - A number of lines in which various activities are

written down as they come up. At the end of the day, the ones that have been completed are checked off.

- A *Records Sheet.* This is the set of raw data needed to produce pertinent reports and graphics. Depending on the objectives, this contains different sets of boxes. Normally, this sheet would include the date, the description, and the number of Pomodoros of effort needed to accomplish a task. This sheet is updated at least once a day, usually at the end of the day.

In the simple examples shown in this book, the Recording, Processing, and Visualizing stages are done directly on the Records Sheet.

☞ Because of typographical constraints, the sheets used in this book show only the entries relating to the topic in question. Simple models of the sheets described here are provided at the end of the book and can be used to practice the technique.

An evolutionary approach to the use of the Pomodoro Technique is provided in the following chapters, oriented to a progressive experimentation with the technique. Clearly, the incremental nature of the technique means that the objectives should be achieved in the order in which they are given here.

OBJECTIVE I:
FIND OUT HOW MUCH
EFFORT AN ACTIVITY REQUIRES

THE TRADITIONAL POMODORO is 30 minutes long: 25 minutes of work plus a 5-minute break. At the beginning of each day, choose the tasks you want to tackle from the Activity Inventory Sheet, prioritize them, and write them down in the To Do Today Sheet (Figure 2).

	TO DO TODAY	
Name: Mark Ross		*the* **Pomodoro** TECHNIQUE
Date: Chicago, July 12, 2018		
	Write article titled "How to Learn Music" (maximum 10 pages)	
	Fine-tune "How to Learn Music" by reading it aloud	
	Condense "How to Learn Music" to three pages	

FIGURE 2: TO DO TODAY SHEET

START THE FIRST POMODORO

Set the Pomodoro for 25 minutes and start the first activity on the To Do Today Sheet. Whoever is using the Pomodoro, whether one person or more, should always be able to see clearly how much time is left (Figure 3).

FIGURE 3: THE TIME REMAINING SHOULD ALWAYS BE VISIBLE

A Pomodoro can't be interrupted: It marks 25 minutes of pure work. A Pomodoro can't be split up: There is no such thing as half a Pomodoro or a quarter of a Pomodoro. The atomic unit of time is a Pomodoro. **(Rule: A Pomodoro is indivisible.)** If a Pomodoro is interrupted by someone or something, that Pomodoro should be considered void, as if it had never been set; then you should make a fresh start with a new Pomodoro. When the Pomodoro rings, mark an "X" next to the activity you've been working on and take a break for 3 to 5 minutes. When the Pomodoro rings, this signals that the current activity is definitely (though temporarily) finished. You're not allowed to keep on working "for just a few more minutes" even if you're convinced that in those few minutes you could complete the task at hand.

	TO DO TODAY	
Name: Mark Ross		*the* **Pomodoro** TECHNIQUE
Date: Chicago, July 12, 2018		

	Write article titled "How to Learn Music" (maximum 10 pages)	x
	Fine-tune "How to Learn Music" by reading it aloud	
	Condense "How to Learn Music" to three pages	

FIGURE 4: THE FIRST POMODORO

The 3- to 5-minute break gives you the time you need to disconnect from your work. This allows your mind to assimilate what's been learned in the last 25 minutes and also gives you a chance to do something good for your health, which will help you do your best during the next Pomodoro. During this break you can stand up and walk around the room, have a drink of water, or fantasize about where you'll go on your next vacation. You can do deep breathing or stretching exercises. If you work with other people, you can swap a joke or two.

During this quick break it's not a good idea to engage in activities that require significant mental effort. For example, don't talk about work-related issues with a colleague, don't write important e-mails or make urgent phone calls, and so on. Doing these kinds of things would block the constructive mental integration that you need to feel alert and ready for the start of the next Pomodoro. You should include these activities in your Activity Inventory and earmark specific Pomodoros for doing them. Clearly, during this break you shouldn't continue thinking about what you've done during the last Pomodoros. Once the break is over, set the Pomodoro to 25 minutes and continue the activity at hand until the next time it rings. Then mark another "X" on the To Do Today Sheet (Figure 5).

TO DO TODAY	
Name: Mark Ross Date: Chicago, July 12, 2018	the *Pomodoro* TECHNIQUE
Write article titled "How to Learn Music" (maximum 10 pages) Fine-tune "How to Learn Music" by reading it aloud	xx
Condense "How to Learn Music" to three pages	

FIGURE 5: THE SECOND POMODORO

Take a 3- to 5-minute break and then start a new Pomodoro.

EVERY FOUR POMODOROS

Every four Pomodoros, stop the activity you're working on and take a longer break, from 15 to 30 minutes.

The 15- to 30-minute break provides an ideal opportunity to tidy your desk, take a trip to the coffee machine, listen to voice mail, check incoming e-mails, or simply rest and do breathing exercises or take a walk. The important thing is not to do anything complex; otherwise your mind won't be able to reorganize and integrate what you've learned, and as a result you won't be able to give the next Pomodoro your best effort. Obviously, during this break you need to stop thinking about what you did during the last Pomodoros.

	TO DO TODAY	
	Name: Mark Ross **Date:** Chicago, July 12, 2018	the *Pomodoro* TECHNIQUE

	Write article titled "How to Learn Music" (maximum 10 pages)	x x x x
	Fine-tune "How to Learn Music" by reading it aloud	
	Condense "How to Learn Music" to three pages	

FIGURE 6: THE END OF THE FIRST SET OF POMODOROS

COMPLETING AN ACTIVITY

Keep on working, Pomodoro after Pomodoro, until the task is finished and then cross it out on the To Do Today Sheet (Figure 7).

	TO DO TODAY	
Name:	Mark Ross	the *Pomodoro* TECHNIQUE
Date:	Chicago, July 12, 2018	
	~~Write article titled "How to Learn Music" (maximum 10 pages)~~	x x x x x
	Fine-tune "How to Learn Music" by reading it aloud	
	Condense "How to Learn Music" to three pages	

FIGURE 7: COMPLETING AN ACTIVITY

Specific cases should be handled with common sense:

- If you finish a task while the Pomodoro is still ticking, the following rule applies: **If a Pomodoro begins, it has to ring**. It's a good idea to take advantage of the opportunity for overlearning, using the remaining portion of the Pomodoro to review or repeat what you've done, make small improvements, and note what you've learned until the Pomodoro rings.
- If you finish an activity in the first 5 minutes of the Pomodoro and feel the task actually was finished during the previous Pomodoro and revision wouldn't be

worthwhile, as an exception to the rule, the current Pomodoro doesn't have to be included in the Pomodoro count.

	TO DO TODAY	
Name: Mark Ross		
Date: Chicago, July 12, 2018		
	~~Write article titled "How to Learn Music" (maximum 10 pages)~~	x x x x x
	~~Fine-tune "How to Learn Music" by reading it aloud~~	x x
	~~Condense "How to Learn Music" to three pages~~	x x x

FIGURE 8: COMPLETING SEVERAL ACTIVITIES

Once the current activity has been completed, move on to the next one on the list and then the next, taking breaks after every Pomodoro and every four Pomodoros (Figure 8).

RECORDING

At the end of every day, the completed Pomodoros can be transferred to a hard-copy archive. As an alternative, it may be more convenient to use an electronic spreadsheet or a database and delete the completed activities from the Activity Inventory Sheet. What you track and record depends on what you want to observe and the kinds of reports you want to generate. The initial aim of tracking and later recording could be simply to present a report with the number of Pomodoros completed per task. In other words, you may want to show the effort expended to accomplish each activity. To do that, you can use the following boxes: the date, the start time, the type of activity, a description of the activity, the actual number of Pomodoros, a short note on the results achieved, and possible room for improvement or problems that may have come up (Figure 9). This initial recording model actually represents the report you want. It's easy to draw it up even on paper.

RECORDS					
Name: <u>Mark Ross</u>				*the* **Pomodoro** TECHNIQUE	
DATE	**TIME**	**TYPE**	**ACTIVITY**	**ACTUAL POMODOROS**	**NOTES**
07/12/2018	8:30	Writing	"How to Learn Music"	5	7 pages
07/12/2018	11:30	Fine-tuning	"How to Learn Music"	2	
07/12/2018	2:00	Condensing	"How to Learn Music"	3	from seven to three pages

FIGURE 9: RECORDS SHEET

How did Mark fill in the time he began an activity if he didn't track it? With the Pomodoro Technique, it's not essential to track the start time for an activity (or for every Pomodoro). What's important is to track the number of Pomodoros actually completed: the real effort. **This point is the key to understanding the Pomodoro Technique.** Since tracking is done at least once a day, remembering and reconstructing the start times for activities isn't difficult; in fact, this kind of recall is a beneficial mental exercise.

☞ A useful technique for remembering start times is to do a rundown of the day beginning with the most recent activity and moving backward to the first one.

IMPROVEMENT

Recording provides an effective tool for people who apply the Pomodoro Technique in terms of self-observation and decision making aimed at process improvement. For example, you can ask yourself how many Pomodoros a week you spend on work activities and on explorative activities, how many Pomodoros you do on an average day of the week, and so on. You also can determine whether the stages in the process are all effective or whether one could be eliminated while you achieve the same results.

For instance, we can see in Figure 9 that it took Mark 10 Pomodoros to write, fine-tune, and condense the article "How to Learn Music." That seems like too many. Mark would like to get the same result with nine Pomodoros or less. Then he would have one or more Pomodoros of free time for other activities. "I'd like to try to write the next article with the same quality and less effort. How? What should I cut out? What activities are really useful? How can I reorganize them to be more effective?"

These are the types of questions that enable people to improve, or at least try to improve, their work or study processes. At the end of the day, the activity of recording (and later looking for ways to improve) should not take more than one Pomodoro.

THE NATURE OF THE POMODORO

The Pomodoro marks the passage of time, and so it is a measure of the dimension of time. It becomes a measure of the dimension of effort when it is combined with the number of people involved in an activity. Depending on this number, we can say that a task was accomplished with a certain number of Person Pomodoros or Pair Pomodoros or Team Pomodoros, where these units measure effort. The quantities of effort relative to different numbers of people are not homogeneous; they can't be added together or compared with one another.

The work of an individual, a pair, or a group represents a different way of combining production factors and implies diverse means of communication. There are no formulas for converting Person Pomodoros to Pair Pomodoros or Team Pomodoros.

☞ Let's say we want to measure the cost of an activity performed by more than one person individually, in pairs, or in teams. By applying a monetary measurement, we can compare and add up the different amounts of effort. For example, take an activity that's achieved by the effort of two Person Pomodoros and three Pair Pomodoros. In terms of effort, these amounts cannot be compared directly or summed in any way. However, by assigning a monetary value for the effort of one Pomodoro, for example, $10.00, we can say that the activity costs $2 \times \$10.00 + 3 \times 2 \times \$10.00 = \$80.00$.

OBJECTIVE II:
CUT DOWN ON INTERRUPTIONS

THE LENGTH OF a Pomodoro—25 minutes—seems short enough to make it possible to resist being distracted by various kinds of interruptions. However, experience shows that once you've started using the Pomodoro Technique, interruptions can become a real problem. That's why an effective strategy is needed to minimize interruptions and progressively increase the number of Pomodoros that can be accomplished consistently without interruptions. There are two kinds of interruptions: internal and external.

INTERNAL INTERRUPTIONS
Even though a Pomodoro lasts only 25 minutes, it won't be easy for everyone to finish the first few Pomodoros without giving in to an immediate need to interrupt the activity at hand: the need to stand up and get something to eat or drink, to make a call that suddenly seems urgent, to look up something on the Internet (it may be related or unrelated to the task at hand), or to check one's e-mails. Finally, we might even need to rethink how we've prioritized this particular activity; we're constantly second-guessing our daily planning or our decisions.

These kinds of distractions, or ways to procrastinate during the activity at hand, are called internal interruptions. They generally disguise our fear of not being able to finish what we're working on the way we want and when we want. Internal interruptions often are associated with having little ability to concentrate.

How can we free ourselves from these internal interruptions? We have to work on two fronts:

1. Make these interruptions clearly visible. Every time you feel a potential interruption coming on, put an apostrophe (') on the sheet where you record your Pomodoros.
2. Make a decision about what to do. You can choose to do one of the following:
   - Write down the new activity on the To Do Today Sheet under "Unplanned & Urgent" if you think it's imminent and can't be put off.
   - Write it down in the Activity Inventory, marking it with a "U" (unplanned); add a deadline if necessary.
   - Intensify your determination to finish the current Pomodoro. Once you've marked the apostrophe, continue working on the task till the Pomodoro rings. (**Rule: Once a Pomodoro begins, it has to ring.**)

The aim is to accept the fact that needs do emerge and shouldn't be neglected. Look at them objectively and if possible reschedule them for another time.

SCENARIO

An example will clarify the dynamic of handling internal interruptions. During the second Pomodoro for writing the article "How to Learn Music," Mark suddenly feels that he has to call his friend Carol to find out when his favorite rock group is giving its next concert. Mark asks himself: "Is this really urgent? Do I have to do it today? No, I can put it off. Maybe an hour or two. Maybe even until tomorrow." Mark puts an apostrophe on the To Do Today Sheet next to the current activity (Figure 10), adds an item to the Activity Inventory for unplanned activities (marked with a "U"—Figure 11), and continues with the Pomodoro.

	TO DO TODAY	
Name: Mark Ross		
Date: Chicago, July 12, 2018		
	Write article titled "How to Learn Music" (maximum 10 pages)	x '
	Fine-tune "How to Learn Music" by reading it aloud	
	Condense "How to Learn Music" to three pages	

FIGURE 10: AN INTERNAL INTERRUPTION

	ACTIVITY INVENTORY	
Name: Mark Ross		*the* **Pomodoro** TECHNIQUE
	...	
u	Call Carol: When's the next rock concert?	
	...	

FIGURE 11: AN UNPLANNED ACTIVITY

Then Mark asks himself: "Does this activity have to be done by tomorrow? No, it just has to be done by the end of the week." Mark adds this deadline in brackets next to the "U" (Figure 12).

	ACTIVITY INVENTORY	
Name: Mark Ross		*the* **Pomodoro** TECHNIQUE
u (July 14)	Call Carol: When's the next rock concert?	
	...	

FIGURE 12: AN UNPLANNED ACTIVITY WITH A DEADLINE

If Mark gets a sudden craving for a pizza 10 minutes later, he'll mark down another apostrophe, but this time he'll note this activity on the To Do Today Sheet under "Unplanned & Urgent" (Figure 13). Then Mark will continue with his Pomodoro.

	TO DO TODAY	
Name: Mark Ross		
Date: Chicago, July 12, 2018		
	Write article titled "How to Learn Music" (maximum 10 pages)	x ' '
	Fine-tune "How to Learn Music" by reading it aloud	
	Condense "How to Learn Music" to three pages	
	UNPLANNED & URGENT	
	Order a pizza	

FIGURE 13: AN URGENT INTERNAL INTERRUPTION

Until this point, the Pomodoro hasn't been interrupted. It's kept on ticking, and Mark has continued working, dealing with interruptions. Clearly, as little time as possible should be spent dealing with interruptions: a few seconds at most. Otherwise the Pomodoro has to be considered interrupted or void. Finally, the Pomodoro rings. Mark records it with an "X" and takes a quick break (Figure 14).

Mark decides to move on to the next Pomodoro. Eight potential interruptions await him during the third Pomodoro, but fortunately, he deals with them all: He classifies one activity as not urgent and records it in the Activity Inventory; he has no choice but to categorize the other interruptions as urgent (Figure 15).

	TO DO TODAY	
Name:	Mark Ross	
Date:	Chicago, July 12, 2018	
	Write article titled "How to Learn Music" (maximum 10 pages)	x '' x
	Fine-tune "How to Learn Music" by reading it aloud	
	Condense "How to Learn Music" to three pages	
	UNPLANNED & URGENT	
	Order a pizza	

FIGURE 14: URGENT INTERNAL INTERRUPTION, SECOND POMODORO

The urgency of the activities listed in Figure 15 might make some people smile, but that's the way Mark perceives them. The point is that with the Pomodoro Technique, lots of useful or fun things to do come up, but we make a conscious decision not to do them during the current Pomodoro.

When we read through the various activities and the urgency we assign to each, we can see how much our minds are moving and how hard it is to keep them still and focus on the activity at hand. Often, the number and variety of attempted internal interruptions are symptoms of our fear of failure to complete the task at hand.

TO DO TODAY	
Name: Mark Ross	
Date: Chicago, July 12, 2018	
Write article titled "How to Learn Music" (maximum 10 pages)	x ' ' x ' ' ' ' ' ' ' '
Fine-tune "How to Learn Music" by reading it aloud	
Condense "How to Learn Music" to three pages	
UNPLANNED & URGENT	
Order a pizza	
Choose a bike to buy	
Read article on learning music in Asia	
Look for July jazz happenings in Chicago on Internet	
Check e-mail	
Order Chinese takeout	
Tidy desk drawers	
Sharpen pencils	

FIGURE 15: SEVERAL URGENT INTERNAL INTERRUPTIONS

It should come as no surprise that many of these distractions later prove to be anything but urgent even to the person who wrote them down. Most likely at the end of the Pomodoro or the activity or the day, several items marked urgent or absolute priority will be handled in different ways:

- They'll be moved to the Activity Inventory. Maybe we can pick out a bike tomorrow.
- They'll be done during longer breaks. That's the time to look up jazz concerts in Chicago in July, for example.
- They'll be deleted. Does Mark really want to order a pizza along with spring rolls and Peking duck? He might even realize that he doesn't want to order anything and will eat at the end of the day.

It's a different mind that reads over those items at the end of a Pomodoro, or a set of four, or at the end of the day. The new perspective is sometimes surprising. Truly urgent tasks are always highlighted on the To Do Today Sheet. The aim of the Pomodoro Technique is to ensure that the current Pomodoro isn't interrupted by these activities. Instead, the following options are available:

- They can be done during the next Pomodoro (but still measured by a Pomodoro) in place of other activities.
- They can be rescheduled during the day in place of other activities.
- They can be moved from Pomodoro to Pomodoro till the end of the day. This helps us gradually learn to recognize what's really urgent.

If and when unplanned urgent activities are done during the day, the relative Pomodoros are marked down in the proper space (Figure 16).

TO DO TODAY	
Name: Mark Ross	
Date: Chicago, July 12, 2018	
Write article titled "How to Learn Music" (maximum 10 pages)	x '' x '''''''''
Fine-tune "How to Learn Music" by reading it aloud	
Condense "How to Learn Music" to three pages	
UNPLANNED & URGENT	
Order a pizza	
Choose a bike to buy	
~~Read article on learning music in Asia~~	x
Look for July jazz happenings in Chicago on Internet	
Check e-mail	
Order Chinese takeout	
Tidy desk drawers	
Sharpen pencils	

FIGURE 16: UNPLANNED ACTIVITY DONE DURING THE DAY

In all the cases discussed so far, the interruptions can be considered to have been handled. Note that the mechanism for handling interruptions consists of inverting the dependency on internal interruptions and consequently making these interruptions depend on the Pomodoros into which we decide to slot them.

If you have to interrupt a Pomodoro because you give in to temptation or something truly urgent comes up, there's only one thing to do: Void the current Pomodoro even if it's about to ring. (**Rule: A Pomodoro is indivisible.**) Then mark an apostrophe where Pomodoros are recorded to keep track of the interrupted Pomodoro. Obviously, you can't mark the unfinished Pomodoro—which didn't actually ring—with an "X," so take a 5 minute break and start with a new Pomodoro.

The next Pomodoro will go better.

☞ The first objective in cutting down on interruptions is to be aware of the number and type of internal interruptions. Observe them, accept them, and schedule them or delete them as the case may be.

EXTERNAL INTERRUPTIONS

People who work in social environments can be interrupted: Your study partner asks you to explain a paragraph or suggests going to a movie after dinner, a phone call isn't filtered by the secretary, a colleague asks you how to compile a report, an e-mail program beeps every time a new message comes in. What should you do?

External interruptions call for the ability to "protect" the ticking Pomodoro. Until now a major effort has been made to eliminate internal interruptions. Now the risk is that someone on the outside will prevent you from having the pleasure of marking an "X" on your To Do Today Sheet.

The main difference between internal and external interruptions is that with the latter we need to interact with other people: We need to communicate. The mechanism for dealing with external interruptions is the same as that for internal ones: Invert the dependency on interruptions and make the interruptions depend on us.

A few examples will clarify what we need to do. Incoming phone calls can be taken by the answering machine, and the messages can be listened to later. E-mails can keep coming in without distracting our attention if you simply deactivate the acoustic signals for incoming messages. If a colleague or study partner comes over, you can politely say you're busy and can't be interrupted. (Some people use humor by saying, "I'm in the middle of a Pomodoro.")

Then tell the person that you'd rather call him or her back in 25 minutes, in a few hours, or tomorrow, depending on how urgent and important the matter is. Speaking from experience, true emergencies that need to be dealt with instantly are rare in real life. A 25-minute or 2-hour delay (four Pomodoros) is almost always possible for activities that are commonly considered urgent. This delay isn't usually detrimental to the person who wants to communicate with you but gives you an enormous advantage in terms of making your mind work effectively, finishing activities the way you want to, and rescheduling urgent tasks. With practice, you'll come to realize how often apparently urgent activities can even be postponed until the next day while still satisfying the person making the request.

Thus, **Protect the Pomodoro** means inform effectively, negotiate quickly to reschedule the interruption, and call back the person who interrupted you as agreed. The Inform, Negotiate, Call Back Strategy enables you to control external interruptions by rescheduling them in a later Pomodoro the same day or another day according to the degree of urgency. The dependency inversion for interruptions lies in this mechanism: We're no longer dependent on interruptions; interruptions depend on us (i.e., the Pomodoros we allocate for calling back).

The feedback from people who start applying the Pomodoro Technique is often the same: They discover that they can have 10 or even 15 external interruptions during a single Pomodoro (25 minutes). If the people doing the interrupting learn that you'll really call them back and are not just putting them off, it won't take long to see our habitual interrupters protecting the Pomodoro too. Many people who work or study with Pomodoro users say they have the feeling that they're dealing with people who appreciate the value of their own time. In operational terms, handling this type of interruption is like dealing with internal interruptions. In this case, too, we work on two fronts:

1. Make these interruptions clearly visible. Every time someone or something tries to interrupt a Pomodoro, put a dash (–) on the sheet where you record your Pomodoros.

2. Make a decision about what to do. You can choose to do one of the following:

- Write down the new activity on the To Do Today Sheet under "Unplanned & Urgent" if it has to be done today, adding the promised deadline in brackets in the left-hand margin.
- Write it down in the Activity Inventory, marking it with a "U" (unplanned); add a deadline in brackets if necessary.
- Intensify your determination to finish the Pomodoro. Once you've marked the dash, continue working on the task until the Pomodoro rings.

This way, you'll achieve the objective of remembering the commitment you made, as well as measuring daily external interruptions, without interrupting the Pomodoro. The following example shows two external interruptions that were handled in different ways during the second Pomodoro of "Write an Article titled 'How to Learn Music'" (Figures 17 and 18).

TO DO TODAY

Name: Mark Ross
Date: Chicago, July 12, 2018

	Write article titled "How to Learn Music" (maximum 10 pages)	x - -
	Fine-tune "How to Learn Music" by reading it aloud	
	Condense "How to Learn Music" to three pages	
	UNPLANNED & URGENT	
(3:40)	E-mail draft of article to Luke	

FIGURE 17: AN UNPLANNED URGENT ACTIVITY

	...	
u (July 13)	Make an appointment with Maestro Neri for interview	
	...	

ACTIVITY INVENTORY

Name: <u>Mark Ross</u>

the **Pomodoro**
TECHNIQUE

FIGURE 18: AN UNPLANNED ACTIVITY WITH A DEADLINE

If a Pomodoro absolutely has to be interrupted because of human weakness or for a real emergency, there's only one thing to do: Void the current Pomodoro even if it's about to ring. (**Rule: A Pomodoro is indivisible.**) Then put a dash where you record Pomodoros to keep track of interrupted Pomodoros and record the description and the deadline for the activity in the Unplanned & Urgent section. Then start the first Pomodoro for the urgent activity.

The next Pomodoro will go better.

☞ The second objective to achieve in order to cut down on interruptions is to be aware of the number and type of external interruptions. Negotiate them and reschedule them depending on the degree of urgency.

SYSTEMATIC INTERRUPTIONS
In applying the Pomodoro Technique, the first tangible consequence of having to deal systematically with internal and

external interruptions is that Pomodoros earmarked for organizational activities will emerge (e-mails, phone calls, meetings,
etc.). The most natural and most common decision is to set aside
one Pomodoro a day (or more if necessary) to take care of urgent
interruptions. The dependency inversion mechanism applied to
protect the current Pomodoro actually serves to turn interruptions into Pomodoros dedicated to forms of communication.

We should emphasize here that Pomodoro users have the following objectives:

- To delay these Pomodoros as long as possible,
  downgrading the degree of apparent urgency and
  increasing the extent to which these activities can be
  controlled and scheduled
- To cut down gradually on the number of Pomodoros
  used for organizing the interruptions that come up
  throughout the day

People who start applying the Pomodoro Technique are
amazed when they measure the Pomodoros spent on work and
study (without unhandled interruptions) and those used for organizational activities (which in part come from dealing with
interruptions). In some teams, members start off with no more
than two to three Pomodoros dedicated to work per day per person; the remaining Pomodoros are spent on meetings, phone
calls, and e-mails.

RECORDING: QUALITATIVE ESTIMATION ERRORS IN PLANNING

Look at the activities recorded daily and marked with a "U" in the Activity Inventory and the ones marked "Unplanned & Urgent" on the To Do Today Sheet. If you do this, during the planning phase you can assess your ability to identify the numbers and types of activities that are most effective in reaching a specific objective. The greater the number of unplanned activities involved, the greater the qualitative error in your initial estimate. Thus, you can measure the unplanned activities done to attain a certain objective. Clearly, you also can include the total number of internal and external interruptions on the Records Sheet to observe them and try to minimize them over time.

OBJECTIVE III:
ESTIMATE THE EFFORT FOR ACTIVITIES

ONCE YOU'VE BEGUN to master the technique and have achieved the first two objectives, you can start working on quantitative estimates. The long-term objective here is to predict the effort that an activity requires.

The Activity Inventory lists all the activities that need to be done. These tasks come from planning, which is needed to identify ways to reach your objectives (e.g., at the beginning of a project) and deal with interruptions. Some activities lose their purpose over time, and so they can be deleted from the inventory. At the start of each day, estimate how many Pomodoros each activity in the inventory will take. Revise previous estimates if necessary. Record the estimated number of Pomodoros on the relative line (Figure 19). The Pomodoro estimate actually represents the number of Pomodoros needed for a certain number of people to accomplish an activity. Thus, this is a measure of effort. However, in the simple examples that follow, the number of Pomodoros always refers to one person.

	ACTIVITY INVENTORY	
	Name: Lucy Banks	
	...	
	Answer questions on thermodynamics in Chap. 4	2
	Repeat laws of thermodynamics aloud to Mark	3
	Summarize laws of thermodynamics in writing	3
	Call Laura: Invite her to the seminar on thermodynamics	
	Call Mark: Give me my laptop back soon!	
	Call Andrew: Buy tickets to concert?	
	E-mail Nick: How do you do Ex. 2, p. 24?	
	...	

FIGURE 19: DAILY ESTIMATE

Estimates always must be based on complete Pomodoros, and so figures such as 5½ Pomodoros aren't allowed. In this case, count six Pomodoros. If an estimate is greater than five to seven Pomodoros, this means that the activity is too complex. It's better to break it down into several activities, estimate those activities separately, and write them down on several lines in the

Activity Inventory. **The rule is: If it takes more than five to seven Pomodoros, break it down.** If you do this, not only do single activities become less complex, but estimates become more accurate. This effect is magnified when the breakdown involves incremental activities, not simply smaller activities. (Incremental activities deliver a little value at a time.)

If the estimate is less than one Pomodoro (e.g., the time it takes to call Laura to invite her to the thermodynamics seminar or call Mark to ask him to give back the laptop), similar activities should be combined till they add up to one Pomodoro of effort. **The rule is: If it takes less than one Pomodoro, add it up.** Thus, there are two options for activities estimated to last less than one Pomodoro:

- Find and combine similar activities from the Activity Inventory until they add up to one Pomodoro of effort (Figure 20).
- Leave the activity without an estimate and indicate that you'll combine it with another activity when you fill in the To Do Today Sheet.

In choosing a strategy, remember that one of the functions of the Activity Inventory is to facilitate the choice of activities To Do Today. Take the first option if the activities in question are very similar or complementary; leave the other tasks without an estimate and combine them later. In any case, the greater the number of useful activities you have in the Activity Inventory, the simpler it will be to choose which strategy to use and how to combine the various tasks.

	ACTIVITY INVENTORY	
	Name: Lucy Banks	*the* Pomodoro TECHNIQUE
	...	
	Answer questions on thermodynamics in Chap. 4	2
	Repeat laws of thermodynamics aloud to Mark	3
	Summarize laws of thermodynamics in writing	3
	Call Laura: Invite her to the seminar on thermodynamics	
	Call Mark: Give me my laptop back soon! Call Andrew: Buy tickets to concert?	1
	E-mail Nick: How do you do Ex. 2, p. 24?	
	...	

FIGURE 20: ACTIVITIES ESTIMATED AT LESS THAN ONE POMODORO

☞ Any changes to the Activity Inventory can be made with a good pencil and an excellent eraser.

AVAILABLE POMODOROS

Now that you have an estimate of the number of Pomodoros for each activity, you can put together a set of activities that doesn't exceed the number of Pomodoros available in a day. Record these available Pomodoros on the To Do Today Sheet; you normally would do this before actually listing the things to do. Figure 21 shows an example of eight Pomodoros available on July 12. Then pick out the tasks to do for the day, combining activities if necessary. (**Rule: If it takes less than one Pomodoro, add it up.**) Write the activities you've chosen in order of priority on the To Do Today Sheet. For each one, every estimated Pomodoro is represented by an empty box (Figure 21).

	TO DO TODAY	
Name: Lucy Banks		*the* Pomodoro TECHNIQUE
Date: Chicago, July 12, 2018		
Available Pomodoros: 8		
	Answer questions on thermodynamics in Chap. 4	☐ ☐
	Repeat laws of thermodynamics aloud to Mark	☐ ☐ ☐
	Summarize laws of thermodynamics in writing	☐ ☐ ☐

FIGURE 21: ESTIMATED POMODOROS

There's no point adding activities beyond the total estimate of eight Pomodoros. If the number of estimated Pomodoros is higher than the number of Pomodoros needed to complete the activities, the remaining number of Pomodoros can be considered only after you're finished. Then you can choose tasks from the inventory to fill in that extra time.

POSSIBLE SCENARIOS

Set the timer and, as always, begin with the first activity on your list. Every time the Pomodoro rings, put an "X" in the first empty box (Figure 22).

FIGURE 22: FIRST POMODORO ESTIMATED AND ACCOMPLISHED

If you finish the activity in the exact number of estimated Pomodoros, cross out the description of the activity (Figure 23).

FIGURE 23: ACTIVITIES DONE IN THE EXACT NUMBER OF ESTIMATED

POMODOROS

If you finish the activity in fewer Pomodoros than you estimated (overestimation error), cross out the description of the activity (Figure 24).

	TO DO TODAY	
Name: Lucy Banks Date: Chicago, July 12, 2018 Available Pomodoros: 8		
	~~Answer questions on thermodynamics in Chap. 4~~	☒ ☒
	~~Repeat laws of thermodynamics aloud to Mark~~	☒ ☒ ☐
	Summarize laws of thermodynamics in writing	☐ ☐ ☐

FIGURE 24: OVERESTIMATION

If you've used up the estimated Pomodoros and need more Pomodoros to finish the task you're working on (quantitative underestimation error), you can do one of two things:

- Continue and mark down the next Pomodoros without taking into account new estimates. Figure 25 shows a case in which another Pomodoro is needed to complete an activity.
- Make a new estimate in Pomodoros and mark these new estimated Pomodoros to the right of the last estimated and completed Pomodoro, using a different color or shape. This way you can highlight the need for second or third estimates and verify relative errors (Figure 26).

FIGURE 25: UNDERESTIMATION

FIGURE 26: SECOND ESTIMATE

As you can see in Figure 27, the summary took Lucy four Pomodoros, three of which were estimated originally (underestimation) and only one of the two which was estimated later (overestimation).

TO DO TODAY

Name: Lucy Banks

Date: Chicago, July 12, 2018

Available Pomodoros: __8__

the Pomodoro

TECHNIQUE

	~~Answer questions on thermodynamics in Chap. 4~~	☒ ☒
	~~Repeat laws of thermodynamics aloud to Mark~~	☒ ☒ ☐
	~~Summarize laws of thermodynamics in writing~~	☒ ☒ ☒ ⊗ ○

FIGURE 27: FINISHING THE ACTIVITY WITH THE SECOND ESTIMATE

Since tasks normally don't last more than seven estimated Pomodoros (**Rule: If it takes more than five to seven Pomodoros, break it down**), there are usually no more than three estimates. All the activities that require a third estimate have to be reconsidered carefully to understand why estimating was so complicated.

RECORDING ESTIMATES

Now that we've introduced the concept of quantitative estimates, the objectives of the reporting system can be more ambitious. New objectives could include the following:

- To measure the accuracy of estimates, analyzing the gap between estimated effort and actual effort (estimation error) for every activity

- To show where more estimates were needed (second or third estimates)

Now the Records Sheet has to be modified. Depending on the case, the report could show estimates, actual effort, and related error. Two simple options for visualizing this information follow (Figures 28 and 29).

			RECORDS			
Name: Lucy Banks						
DATE	**TIME**	**TYPE**	**ACTIVITY**	**ESTIMATE**	**REAL**	**DIFF.**
7/12/2018	10:00	Study	Answer questions on thermodynamics in Chap. 4	2	2	0
7/12/2018	11:30	Repeat	Repeat laws of thermodynamics aloud to Mark	3	2	-1
7/12/2018	2:00	Summarize	Summarize laws of thermodynamics in writing	3	4	1

FIGURE 28: FIRST ESTIMATE ONLY

There are many possible ways to present the results that you're tracking. The complexity of the reporting objectives is not too high, and reports can be obtained directly from the Records Sheet with just a few calculations done by hand. The more

complex the calculations are, the more you'll want to make use
of databases, spreadsheets, and ad hoc software applications. Remember: Always make recording activity as simple as possible.

			RECORDS				
Name: Lucy Banks							
DATE	TIME	TYPE	ACTIVITY	ESTIMATE	REAL	DIFF. I	DIFF. II
7/12/2018	10:00	Study	Answer questions on thermodynamics in Chap. 4	2	2	0	
7/12/2018	11:30	Repeat	Repeat laws of thermodynamics aloud to Mark	3	2	1	
7/12/2018	2:00	Summarize	Summarize laws of thermodynamics in writing	3 + 2	4	-1	1

FIGURE 29: FIRST AND SECOND ESTIMATES

☞ The first objective of improving quantitative estimates
is to eliminate the third estimate and keep the overall
margin of error small. The next objective is to eliminate
the second estimate, again keeping the overall margin of
error small. The final objective is to reduce the margin of
error in the first estimate.

MANAGING EXPLORATION

Not every activity can be estimated. At the outset of a new project or study activity, it's especially beneficial to spend time on exploration: Look for new sources, get an idea of the structure of the texts you have to study or consult, and define your objectives more clearly. To guide exploration, it's worthwhile to apply the concept of time-boxing. Decide on a number of Pomodoros for completing your exploration. When these Pomodoros are finished, set up your real work plan or start on a specific activity or decide if you want to keep exploring and what direction you want to take.

OBJECTIVE IV:
MAKE THE POMODORO
MORE EFFECTIVE

WHEN YOU CAN use the Pomodoro systematically without interruptions and you start to master estimating, you can evolve the Pomodoro Technique even further.

THE STRUCTURE OF THE POMODORO
The first evolution has to do with the structure of the Pomodoro. The first 3 to 5 minutes of each Pomodoro can be used to repeat briefly what you've learned since the beginning of the activity (not just the last Pomodoro) and then to imprint this in your memory. The last 3 to 5 minutes of a Pomodoro can be used to review quickly what you've done (if possible, with an effect-cause procedure, starting from the last activities and going back to your initial motivations).

These changes don't require variations in the length of the 25-minute Pomodoro. The enhanced awareness of time you can achieve by using the Pomodoro will enable you to sense physiologically the 3- to 5-minute intervals mentioned above. If you have a hard time doing this, it may be a sign that you haven't mastered the basic technique.

☞ The last few minutes of the Pomodoro allow you to review what you've done. If you want to check the quality and methods of your work to pinpoint potential improvement, you should plan one or two Pomodoros for this task. (Quicker observations are made daily during the recording Pomodoro.)

THE STRUCTURE OF THE POMODORO SET

There is a second evolution that has to do with the four-Pomodoro set. As was described above, the first Pomodoro in a set of four, or part of this first Pomodoro, can be used to repeat what you've done so far. Similarly, all or part of the last Pomodoro in the set can be used to review what you've accomplished. Repetition and revision activities are more effective if you do them aloud or by talking with a partner or a member of your team. Systematic repetition and revision stimulates the effects of *overlearning*, facilitating the acquisition of new information.

OBJECTIVE V:
SET UP A TIMETABLE

THERE ARE A number of reasons you should never underestimate the importance of defining and respecting a timetable:

- A timetable sets a limit. Limits (when they're truly understood as inviolable) help us be concrete, do things. They motivate us to do our best to complete the tasks before us within a set period. The same thing happens when the Pomodoro rings.

- A timetable delineates the separation between work time and free time; the latter is best defined as time set aside for non-goal-oriented or unplanned activities. This leisure time is fuel for our minds. Without it, creativity, interest, and curiosity are lost and we run ourselves down until our energy is depleted. Without gas, the engine won't run.

- A timetable measures the results of the day. Once we've written up the To Do Today Sheet, our goal is to carry out the activities listed on it with the highest possible quality within the set time frame. If time runs out and these activities aren't done, we try to

understand what went wrong. In the meantime, we
have an invaluable piece of information: how many
Pomodoros we managed to work that day.

With the Pomodoro Technique, figuring out how much time
is wasted isn't important; how many Pomodoros we've accomplished is. The next day, keep that number in mind when you
are deciding how many Pomodoros are available and write down
activities to fill only those Pomodoros.

The main risk with the timetable is underestimating how important it is; it's easy to fall into the trap of not respecting it. For
example, let's say it's 3 p.m. You've lost time during the day, and
you know you haven't produced as much as you could have or as
much as you expected. Therefore, you tell yourself: "Today I'll
work late to make up for lost time." A combination of heroism
and guilt makes you breach the limit set by the timetable; as a
result, your performance is ineffective tonight, then tomorrow
night, and then the night after that. The more the timetable is
systematically prolonged, the more the overall results will di-
minish. Guilt intensifies. Why? Isn't playing the hero enough?
Don't the hours sacrificed in the name of work assuage the guilt?

Actually, what emerges is a dangerous vicious circle: The
timetable is protracted, fatigue increases, productivity drops,
and the timetable again is protracted. First and foremost, an effective timetable must be respected. A timetable can be made
up of a series of time slots, each dedicated to a different type of
activity. Respecting a timetable means developing immunity to
the Five More Minutes Syndrome. When a time slot ends, just
as when the Pomodoro rings, all activity stops. No matter how
much time is still left on your Pomodoro, the same rule applies:

The Timetable Always Overrides the Pomodoro. Second, an effective timetable has to allow for the free time that you need to recuperate.

> ☞ It may happen that an important deadline comes up and you find yourself having to work longer hours. This overtime can be factored into your timetable to increase productivity momentarily. Typically, to achieve positive results and avoid the risk of the vicious circle mentioned above, you shouldn't work overtime for more than five days in a row. Establish an ad hoc timetable for this period and set aside a recovery period to deal with the drop in productivity that inevitably will follow.

THE BEST-CASE SCENARIO

Let's use the following timetable as an example: 8:30–1:00, 2:00–5:30. It's 8:30. Albert winds up the first Pomodoro of the day. He might use this Pomodoro to look over all the things he did the day before and to skim over the Activity Inventory and fill in the To Do Today Sheet, which also will include this planning activity. In this same organizational Pomodoro, Albert checks that everything on his desk is in place and ready and tidies it if it's not. The Pomodoro rings, "X," break.

Another Pomodoro begins: the first operational Pomodoro. And so it goes for two more Pomodoros. The four-Pomodoro set is over, followed by a longer break. Despite the fact that he wants to keep working, Albert decides to take a bit more downtime in anticipation of the intense workday ahead. Instead of taking only the minimum 15-minute break, he takes 20 minutes. He then winds up a new Pomodoro. He continues for a total of four Pomodoros and then checks his watch. It's 12:53. He has just enough time to tidy his desk again, put away any papers that need to be filed, and check that the To Do Today Sheet is filled out clearly and properly before he goes to lunch.

By 2:00 Albert is at his desk again. He winds up the Pomodoro and gets back to work. He doesn't take much of a break between one Pomodoro and the next.

But after four rings he starts feeling tired. He still has a few more Pomodoros to go. He wants to get a good rest, and he tries to disconnect as best he can by taking a walk. Thirty minutes later, Albert winds up a new Pomodoro. It rings, "X," break. Albert sets aside the last Pomodoro to look over what he achieved during the day, fill in the Records Sheet, jot down some comments on areas for improvement, make notes on the To Do Today Sheet for the next day, and tidy his desk. The Pomodoro rings. Quick break. Albert looks at his watch. It's 5:27. He straightens any papers that are out of place and puts the activity sheets in order. At 5:30 free time begins.

Two comments on this scenario:

- The operational Pomodoros never coincide with the number of work/study hours. With eight hours of work/study, 2 Pomodoros are earmarked for organizational activities (one hour) and 12 (six hours) for operational activities.

- The time that goes by is always a secondary factor with the Pomodoro Technique. If there are no un-handled interruptions, the end of the morning or afternoon will be determined simply by the succession of Pomodoros. The timetable is reinforced by sets of Pomodoros. It doesn't matter what time it is, because our guide is the sequence of Pomodoros with their respective breaks. In terms of the timetable in this example, we have [1+3],[4]:[4],[1+1].

A SCENARIO WITH INTERRUPTIONS

Let's say it's the second Pomodoro in the second set of the scenario described above.

Albert gets interrupted and can't deal with the interruption. That can happen. The Pomodoro is void. Finally, Albert is free to get back to work again. He checks the time. It's 12:20. In a few seconds he reorganizes the last session; at this point there's only one Pomodoro left to do. He still takes a quick break before going on to the next Pomodoro. In fact, he decides to take a bit more time to try to find his focus. When he feels ready, Albert winds up the Pomodoro and starts the second Pomodoro in the set. (The first one was interrupted.) In the afternoon, at the end of the third set of four Pomodoros, Albert feels that he needs more than a 3- to 5-minute break. He decides to take a half-hour walk. Before going out, he quickly modifies the last set, which was originally two Pomodoros long, to just one organizational Pomodoro. If there's extra time, he'll tidy his desk and check his incoming e-mails. Albert gets back from his walk at 4:47. He winds up the Pomodoro, it rings, "X," break. Free time.

OPTIMIZING YOUR TIMETABLE

A workday contains several Pomodoros. How should you organize them to make the day more effective? Optimizing your work schedule is the result of a continual process of observation and feedback. The objective is to reinforce the concept of a regular succession of activity as much as possible.

For people who have an entire day to study, an initial timetable might be 8:30–12:30, 1:30–5:30. This consists of two sets made up of four and three Pomodoros, respectively, in the morning and two sets consisting of four and three Pomodoros, respectively, in the afternoon: [4],[3]:[4],[3]. The sets determine when to take breaks.

The Pomodoros within each set can be organized even further. For example, you could earmark the first Pomodoro in the first session for planning the day and the following three for studying new topics, along with the next two Pomodoros from the second set. The last Pomodoro in the second group is set aside for checking and answering e-mails, listening to voice mail, and calling classmates if necessary. This is a way to respond effectively to possible interruptions intercepted during the morning. The first Pomodoro of the third set is for looking over what you did in the morning. The next three Pomodoros are to spend on studying. The first two Pomodoros of the fourth set are used to revise what you've learned today and in the last few days. The last Pomodoro of the day is used for tracking and analyzing data. Thus, your timetable looks something like this: [1+3],[2+1]:[1+3],[2+1].

The basic assumptions with this study schedule are that

people are usually more productive in the morning and that work done in the afternoon hours just after lunch is not very effective. Clearly, these assumptions are subjective. Why do we refer to an initial timetable? Because by gathering information on how they work/how they're working, in other words by tracking metrics of completed Pomodoros and other indicators every day, students can learn to pinpoint which set of Pomodoros is most productive for studying, revising, or being creative. Knowing this, they can consciously modify their study schedule, starting earlier or later, extending certain sets and reducing others, and learning to know themselves better.

Here's the key to organizing a timetable: Make conscious decisions about how to set it up. Up to this point, sets of four Pomodoros have been used because this amount usually is considered the most effective. But you also can use longer or shorter sets lasting, say, three or five Pomodoros. At the end of the set comes a 15- to 30-minute break. To be effective, a timetable should be destined to change over time, and it can be made up of sets of differing numbers of Pomodoros, giving preference to those that last four Pomodoros.

☞ Experience teaches you that when the seasons change, your timetable needs to change too.

OBJECTIVE VI:
DEFINE YOUR OWN PERSONAL
IMPROVEMENT OBJECTIVE

U P TO THIS POINT, this book has described the basic Pomodoro Technique. Until now, by means of simple tracking and recording activities and with very little processing, we've come up with useful reports on effort per activity and on errors in qualitative or quantitative estimates. Naturally, if we want to improve, the reporting objectives will change over time. Of course, it wouldn't be useful to track and record every possible metric; we should do that only for the ones that enable us to observe what we want to consolidate or improve.

The Pomodoro Technique was conceived to be flexible in the face of these kinds of changes. To make tracking and recording new metrics possible, we have to modify the different sheets, as was shown in the previous chapters. While making these alterations, it's essential to keep in mind some key criteria that will preserve the adaptive capability of the technique.

In order of importance:

1. Always remember that using technology entails an increase in complexity as a result of the relative

learning curve and less flexibility compared with
paper, pencil, and eraser.

2. Keep tracking at the lowest possible level of complexity (even delegating small tasks to recording). Choose
simple tools for this activity: Using paper, pencil, and
eraser serves as a useful mental exercise.

3. Keep the recording simple by using the tools best
suited to the complexity you have to manage. Before
turning to a spreadsheet or a database, see if there's
a more effective way to do recording with paper,
pencil, and eraser. Before using ad hoc software, see
if there's a more effective way to do recording with a
spreadsheet or a database.

4. If processing and visualizing become difficult, complex, and repetitive, you have to ask yourself if all
the metrics you're observing are really necessary. If
that turns out to be the case, you should consider
using spreadsheets, a database, or an ad hoc software
program. A simple Excel sheet can readily handle
operations such as reclassifying activities by type,
filtering activities by word, grouping, and applying
calculations to selected activities.

5. Imagination is the most powerful tool for preventing
complexity from growing.

For example, earlier in the book we looked at a case with a
single objective: writing an article titled "How to Learn Music."
This objective is achieved by means of a series of tasks. But you
might find yourself having to consider a number of objectives to
achieve simultaneously. How do you distinguish between them?

Depending on the circumstances, you can change the way you write the description so that you can highlight the objective (Figure 30). Another option is to include a new box labeled "Objectives" in the Activity Inventory, on the To Do Today Sheet, and on the Records Sheet where you can write down a description of the objective or an abbreviation or code that stands for it. To calculate the total effort expended to achieve a particular objective, add up the effort it took to do the related activities.

	TO DO TODAY	
Name: Mark Ross		*the* Pomodoro TECHNIQUE
Date: Chicago, July 12, 2018		
	"How to Learn Music": write article (maximum 10 pages)	
	"How to Learn Music": fine-tune by reading aloud	
	"How to Learn Music": condense to three pages	

FIGURE 30: TO DO TODAY SHEET

You might want to calculate how long it takes to reach certain objectives or perform particular activities. To do this, you simply measure the time from the date of completion back to the date when you wrote in or assigned the activity. Since you already have the completion date for the activity (on the To Do Today Sheet), in the first case you'll need to track the date you slotted that activity into the Activity Inventory; in the second case, you'll track the date you wrote on the To Do Today Sheet.

On the Records Sheet you can track Pomodoros of effort over
several days for the same activity.

> ☞ In any case, choosing which metrics to track and record
> has to be subordinate to the choice of improvement ob-
> jectives. In this case, the metrics system will grow in-
> crementally on the basis of real need, keeping tracking
> complexity to a minimum.

REACHING YOUR
TEAM GOALS

APPLYING
THE POMODORO TECHNIQUE
ON A TEAM

SCIENTIFIC EVIDENCE SUGGESTS that ancient humans started hunting for meat two million years ago. I wonder about the day the first ancient human put aside their pride and asked other people for help. After all, large animals tend to be fierce and difficult prey to hunt on your own.

Most of the goals we want to reach nowadays are difficult or impossible to achieve on our own too. We need somebody else's help to be successful. For instance, our partners, our families, our teams at work, people we have worked with for years, or people we work with only on occasion. Working on a team has allowed us to evolve and acquire the knowledge needed to explore distant planets or understand our own DNA.

I try to imagine that team of ancient humans' first attempts to hunt a large animal. They would not have been successful right away. I can picture them standing in a circle around the prey, each person attacking it individually—violent attempts to kill the beast, which appear haphazard and badly coordinated. I imagine the prey's mocking sneer when it realizes it has resolved the problem of lunch.

ALL TOO OFTEN, TEAMS BECOME PREY TO THEIR GOALS

When we work on a team, goals tend to be more complicated to reach. The more complicated the goals, the more unexpected and urgent the related activities will be, and, in turn, the more destructive the delays and the interruptions will become.

As the complexity of the goal increases, so does the need to coordinate with more people. And the more people who are involved in the process—team members, external consultants, and providers—the more interruptions and delays there will be.

If we as a team lack a time-management strategy—a strategy that helps our team behave effectively when time becomes an issue we have to manage—the team members will end up feeling anxious and afraid.

Let's say you need to deliver a sales report to your manager by the end of the day. All the members of your team are responsible for completing one related activity: Angela is in charge of analyzing data—a very time-consuming activity—and Marc is in charge of getting feedback from your best customers. You and your team planned everything. The goal is feasible. But something is not working as expected. Angela is not at her desk. Someone called her and she was not able to manage the interruption. Marc is having difficulties contacting some clients but he does not let you know. Instead he works harder.

This report was really important and you trusted your team to deliver. How do you think you will react at 5:00 when Angela and Marc explain why they are unable to deliver what they had agreed on? Will you trust them in the future? What makes this situation more unfortunate is that both Angela and Marc acted in good faith; they just did not have an effective time-management strategy in place.

Situations like these create frustration. Anxiety contaminates the team's mood. Feelings of resentment can arise. Trust between team members can start to break down as members blame one another. Conflicts emerge. We end up moving in circles around our goal, accusing and distrusting others, until we burn out, enveloped in an atmosphere of tension, anxiety, and frustration.

When our team gets to this point, we are officially food on our prey's plate.

HOW CAN THE POMODORO TECHNIQUE HELP A TEAM REACH ITS GOALS?

By using the Pomodoro Technique, we want to be able to deliver that sales report by 5:00 with no stress, with no friction, and to the satisfaction of the whole team.

There are several benefits to applying a time-management strategy like the Pomodoro Technique to your team. It can:

- Reduce friction between team members
- Reduce the need for unnecessary meetings
- Protect the team from interruptions
- Help the team complete its goals and activities on time

In the following chapters in this section of the book, we will learn how a team can get the benefits offered by the Pomodoro Technique.

To do that, we will have to adapt and expand the tools and the process of the technique. The timer and the various sheets are the tools. Using the timer and the sheets to reach a goal defines the process. A process answers the question "What do we do, when?" For instance, what do we do when the Pomodoro rings or when there is an interruption? Rules such as "If it takes more than five to seven Pomodoros, break it down" or practices such as the "Inform, Negotiate, Call Back Strategy" support the process.

We will start by considering how to adapt the tools of the technique to a team. Then we will focus on new rules and practices for improving productivity by applying the technique. Ready, set, go!

ADAPTING THE TOOLS OF
THE TECHNIQUE TO A TEAM

THE POMODORO TECHNIQUE has six objectives:

1. Find out how much effort an activity requires
2. Cut down on interruptions
3. Estimate the effort required for activities
4. Make the Pomodoro more effective
5. Set up a timetable
6. Define your own personal improvement objective

In the Reaching Your Individual Goals section, I have demonstrated how to achieve these objectives while working alone. But I often visit teams that are interested in improving their productivity too. Many people have asked me how they can apply the Pomodoro Technique to fit their teams' needs. How do the tools of the technique need to be adapted? I am pleased to be part of your team now and to be able to answer your questions. Let's begin.

DOES EACH MEMBER OF THE TEAM HAVE THEIR OWN POMODORO, OR IS THERE A POMODORO FOR THE WHOLE TEAM?

Each microteam has and manages its own Pomodoro. The rule is **One Microteam, One Pomodoro.**

WHAT IS A MICROTEAM?

A microteam is any number of people working on an activity at a certain time.

For example, a team made up of three people needs to reach a goal. At any particular moment, two people might work on a certain activity together while the third team member works on another activity. During that time, the team is organized into two microteams (Figure 31).

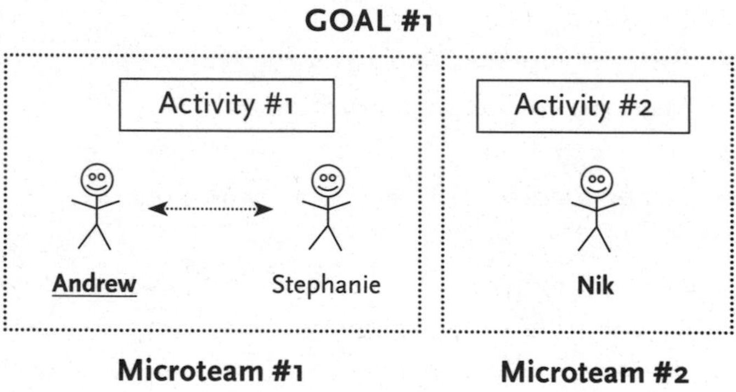

FIGURE 31: MICROTEAMS

In all these diagrams, the underlined name indicates the person responsible for the team reaching a specific *goal*. The bold names indicate the person responsible for completing a certain *activity*. This person is also in charge of the microteam working on that activity. The double-headed dotted arrow indicates interaction between people.

Each activity is carried out by a microteam. A microteam can range in size from one person to all the members of the team. One person on the microteam is always responsible for that activity and in charge of the microteam working on it.

GOAL #1

Activity #1

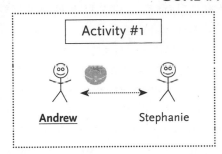

Andrew   Stephanie

Microteam #1

Activity #2

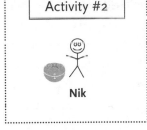

Nik

Microteam #2

GOAL #2

Activity #3

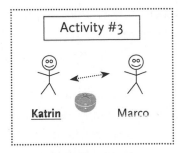

Katrin   Marco

Microteam #3

Activity #4

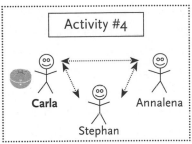

Carla   Annalena

Stephan

Microteam #4

FIGURE 32: GOALS AND MICROTEAMS

Figure 32 shows the number of Pomodoros a team of eight is using at a given point in the day. The team is working on two goals. The first goal has three people working on it: one microteam of two people and one microteam of one person. The second goal has five people working on it: one microteam of two people and another of three people. In accordance with the **One Microteam, One Pomodoro** rule, each of the activities that a microteam is working on has its own Pomodoro.

WHY NOT HAVE ONE POMODORO FOR ALL THE MEMBERS OF THE TEAM?

Breaks are one of the most vital elements of the Pomodoro Technique. They allow our minds the time to process the information that has been acquired and encourage solutions. Breaks become even more important when working on teams. Effective interactions among team members require people to be open, to listen, and to focus. A failure to take adequate breaks can mean that team members feel more stressed and are less able to engage in effective interactions with the rest of the team.

It is not possible to assign a fixed time for the breaks, either between Pomodoros or between blocks of four Pomodoros. At the end of a Pomodoro, one microteam may feel ready to start the next one after just two minutes. Meanwhile, another microteam might need a five-minute break.

Each microteam must be free to decide how long the break will be. Each microteam has a different rhythm, performs a different type of activity, and is made up of different kinds of people, and the members of each team interact in different ways. **Only the microteam's members know how much time they need in order to feel ready to begin the next Pomodoro.**

The "synchronized Pomodoro"—one timer for the entire team, one per microteam, or one per person started at the same time, as if in a production line—does not allow each individual to take the time they need to be able to interact effectively with their team members. Any attempts by teams to work in lockstep force people to ignore their individual needs.

> ☞ Another reason to advise against the "synchronized Pomodoro" is the need to manage interruptions effectively. If Microteam #3 is interrupted by an urgent phone call and cannot successfully manage the break, it would make no sense to stop all the other microteams and void the entire team's Pomodoro.

HOW CAN WE ARRANGE FOR EVERYONE TO ATTEND A MEETING?

The team timetable makes it possible to plan events that involve the whole team: meetings and shared breaks.

Each microteam decides when to start its own Pomodoro and how long the breaks will be. However, regardless of how many minutes are left on each microteam's Pomodoro, it is useful to apply this rule: **The Timetable Always Overrides the Pomodoro.**

The need for shared breaks or meetings attended by the entire team can be met by assigning these activities to time slots in the team timetable:

- Every day from 11:30 a.m. to 11:45 a.m.: Team Break in the second floor kitchen
- Every Friday from 3 p.m. to 5 p.m.: Team Meeting in room #401

☞ Who should draw up and update the team timetable? This is the responsibility of the team members.

WHO SETS THE POMODORO? WHO MAKES THE ESTIMATES? WHO RECORDS THE POMODOROS?

The person in charge of the microteam is responsible for a series of actions and decisions:

- Setting the Pomodoro—this person will physically start the Pomodoro
- Deciding how to organize the structure of the Pomodoro—how to use the first or the last 5 minutes of the Pomodoro
- Putting an "X" on the To Do Today sheet for each completed Pomodoro
- Deciding how to manage interruptions when they occur
- Deciding how long breaks will last, keeping in mind the needs of the microteam members
- Recording the Pomodoros carried out in the course of the day by the microteam they are in charge of

All these actions and decisions strengthen that person's sense of responsibility with regard to the activity to be completed.

DO WE NEED TO MODIFY THE POMODORO TECHNIQUE SHEETS?

Let's look, one by one, at how and why to adapt the various sheets related to the Pomodoro Technique when working on a team.

ADAPTING THE TO DO TODAY SHEET

The only change you need to make when you are in charge of a microteam is to add the name of the person or people who are working with you.

	TO DO TODAY	
	Name: Marco	the *Pomodoro* TECHNIQUE
	Date: Los Angeles, September 20, 2018	
	~~Collect the data for the sales report~~	M: X
	~~Check the data for the sales report~~	MS: X X
	Prepare the sales report	MAK: X

FIGURE 33: TO DO TODAY SHEET

Figure 33 shows Marco's To Do Today sheet. Marco is working on delivering the monthly sales report: this is his goal for the week. From his records, we see that Marco has completed the activity "Collect the data for the sales report" in one Pomodoro; together with Stephan, he completed the activity "Check the data for the sales report" in two Pomodoros. Finally, he worked with Annalena and Katrin on the activity "Prepare the sales report," which took one Pomodoro.

ADAPTING THE RECORDS SHEET

When working in teams, the Records Sheet explicitly shows the estimated effort and the actual effort expended in terms of person Pomodoros:

RECORDS						*the* Pomodoro TECHNIQUE	
DATE	TIME	TYPE	ACTIVITY	ESTIMATE	REAL	DIFF. I	DIFF. II
9/20/2018	10:00	Writing	Prepare the sales report	2P 3p	5P 3p	3p —	

FIGURE 34: RECORDS SHEET

For example, the Records Sheet in Figure 34 shows us two things. Marco had estimated that the work to carry out the activity "Prepare the sales report" would require two Pomodoros for a microteam of three people (2P 3p). We also see that in fact that microteam required five Pomodoros to complete the activity.

There is only one Records Sheet. The same sheet is shared by all team members. At the end of the day, each team member responsible for an activity will fill in data related to their microteam's work that day.

ADAPTING THE ACTIVITY INVENTORY

The Activity Inventory requires some simple modifications when working in teams:

- Adding a column with the person responsible for the activity
- Recording in the estimate column the number of Pomodoros that a particular number of people in a microteam will require to complete a particular activity

The person responsible for the activity is also in charge of the estimate for the activity.

	ACTIVITY INVENTORY		*the* Pomodoro TECHNIQUE
NOTES	**ACTIVITY**	**ESTIMATE**	**PERSON RESPONSIBLE**
	...		
	Prepare the slides to present the new product	4p 2p	Katrin
	...		

FIGURE 35. ACTIVITY INVENTORY

In the example shown in Figure 35, Katrin is responsible for the activity "Prepare the slides to present the new product," and estimates that four Pomodoros of two people will be needed.

SIMPLE PRACTICES
TO GET YOUR TEAM STARTED

I N THE PREVIOUS chapter we saw how to adapt the tools of the Pomodoro Technique—the timers and the various sheets—to work in a team. When it comes to working in a team, we need new rules and practices to adapt the Pomodoro Technique process as well.

If I were asked what I'd suggest to a team that is starting to apply the Pomodoro Technique, I would recommend the following two simple practices, which can be applied immediately.

POMODORO ROTATIONS

This practice goes back to the first applications of the Pomodoro Technique to teams in the late 1990s: With a defined frequency—usually every one, two, or four Pomodoros—one of the members of your microteam switches places with a member of another microteam. The people leading the activities are the only ones who cannot switch places. One by one, each of the members of a microteam switches places with a member of other microteams.

I know that people tend to resist switching from a microteam they are used to. "Isn't it an interruption during work? How do we coordinate so that we can smoothly switch microteam members? Won't it take us longer to finish? Won't it interrupt the flow?" It might seem counterintuitive, but rotating the members of your microteam **systematically** can help you complete your activity more effectively. Each person who comes into the microteam might bring new ideas and different solutions.

When applied routinely, this practice makes it possible to:

- Share knowledge
- Share and improve the team's skills
- Increase the interchangeability of team members
- Keep the team up to date with the current status of the goals and avoid needless meetings

A little common sense will enable the team members to rotate smoothly between microteams, even as frequently as every Pomodoro. The Pomodoro of Microteam #1 has just rung. Katrin is responsible for the activity and expected Stephan from Microteam #2 to rotate with Marco, whom she has just worked with. Microteam #2 is in the middle of their Pomodoro. But Microteam #3 is two minutes away from taking their break. Katrin can choose to wait and ask Stephanie from Microteam #3 to rotate instead of Stephan. It is not necessary to synchronize the timers to implement the rotations. Communication and the ability to adapt will turn what seem like impediments to rotations into opportunities to share knowledge and improve skills.

☞ This practice **must** be chosen by the team members. Forcing or imposing rotations can be frustrating for those who are subjected to it.

SNAP YOUR POMODORO

We have been implementing this practice on my team for a number of years. When the Pomodoro rings, we take a photo. Of what? Of something that shows exactly what our microteam has done during that Pomodoro. One photo per Pomodoro. We often snap things that we did not understand or manage to resolve in that Pomodoro. Or we take a photo of a result that we have achieved.

At the end of the day we have a timeline with a photo for every Pomodoro completed by each microteam. This is not just helpful for simplifying and reducing recording time. It is particularly helpful because it lets us reconstruct weeks of work in just a few minutes; having a visual overview helps to find solutions.

WHY TEAMS NEED
MORE ADVANCED PRACTICES

I STARTED APPLYING the Pomodoro Technique to teams as a coach in the late 1990s. This came about quite by chance. The team consisted of roughly ten software developers from a bank based in Milan. At that time, I worked as a consultant for companies with teams that wanted to improve their software development process. My task was to enable team members to find solutions to problems on their own. To do this, I assigned the team members a lot of material to study. Soon, though, a problem emerged: *When should I study? How do I do it effectively? And without fear and anxiety?* I knew those questions well, and during a break I casually mentioned how I had resolved them: with the timer, 25 minutes, the To Do Today and the Activity Inventory sheets, and so on. Some questions followed, and then we went back to work. But the following month, the team members asked me a question that I didn't know how to answer: *How can we apply the Pomodoro to our team?*

A variety of anxieties and fears lay behind that question. The team was always late in delivering software features. On average, their estimates were off by 400 percent—a feature estimated to take one month to deliver actually took five. Unsurprisingly, their manager had stopped trusting them. The pressure on that team was high. And working under these conditions led to mistakes, or bugs as we say in the software world. Often the manager would barge into the team's open space, tell them to stop all activities immediately, and order them to correct a bug that had been noticed by an internal user or a bank customer. The whole team would then drop everything to correct the bug. It was often necessary to work overtime and even on weekends. Having to deal with bugs meant that no one managed to work on the goals set for the week, which led to new delays and more inaccurate estimates, new frustrations, and even more pressure for everyone.

Thanks to that team in Milan, you can now read this book. The members of that team shared their success at conferences and in blog posts. They were the ones who started the viral process of spreading this technique that has over time been passed on to thousands of other teams around the world and that today has now reached you.

Although the experience of that team in Milan seems extreme, working on a team often leads to difficulties delivering on time, big estimation errors, moments of unbearable stress, and a lack of trust from management or clients. Sometimes an activity is so complex that the microteam simply cannot complete it. Often interruptions from colleagues and clients overwhelm the team. Other times, a microteam cannot complete an activity because of a bottleneck—for instance, when they have to stand by and wait for another microteam to complete an activity before they can resume their own work. All this can happen, and much more. Frustrating and stressful situations such as these often contaminate a team's mood, lowering productivity and bringing the whole team to a standstill.

HOW CAN THE POMODORO TECHNIQUE HELP A TEAM MANAGE COMPLEXITY, INTERRUPTIONS, AND BOTTLENECKS?

In the following chapters you will find my "best practices" for using the Pomodoro Technique with a team to resolve and avoid the frustrating situations I have described. As a coach, my experience with the team in Milan prompted me to start collecting, evolving, and structuring successful practices that could be repeated by other teams. I have developed and tested a number of these practices over almost 20 years. I have applied them with teams of different sizes, skills, and levels of experience. For me, each of these practices is linked to a particular team—to its anxieties and fears and to its achievements. I hope you find them as useful as I have.

THE PRACTICE OF THE COUNTER

M Y HEROES HERE in Berlin are the guys at the Notebook Lounge. They fix computers. Their shop is surprisingly small. When you walk in, you see a lounge with comfy couches to your left. In front of you there is a bar. Behind the counter, there is a team member who is ready to deal with your emergency. Behind him or her is a black curtain. You cannot see what is beyond, but that is where they are saving your computer's life.

Interruptions are one of the most common and expensive problems for teams. Giving in to one single interruption can hold up the work of the whole team. The Practice of the Counter shows how the Pomodoro and a timetable can help the team to manage interruptions. The most fascinating lesson of this practice is that interruptions can be turned into an opportunity to share knowledge and work more effectively. The day I entered my heroes' shop, I recognized several similarities to the practice I have applied many times in the past and that I am now going to describe.

PROBLEM

A team is working on their goals but is overwhelmed by requests for support from various stakeholders: colleagues, clients, consultants, managers, and suppliers. All want immediate answers. Team members repeatedly give in to interruptions, which affects the productivity of the whole team.

SOLUTION

The Practice of the Counter enables the team to protect itself from a high number of external interruptions and to share knowledge among team members.

To show how this practice can be applied, let us imagine the team we are coaching is made up of eight people. They could organize themselves in the following way:

- Create a physical barrier, or counter, to restrict access to the area where the microteams are at work. This team should not be visible to the people requesting support. I have never used a real curtain, but the effect you want to create is the same. To emphasize this effect, from here forward I will call this team the "team behind the curtain."
- Create the "team at the counter"—one or more microteams whose role is to deal with people who need support and manage their requests. In my experience, with an eight-person team, the perfect microteam size is two people. In the example shown in Figure 36, Katrin and Marco form one microteam to work at the counter.

☞ Supporting a customer's request is usually seen as an activity for one person. In order to provide a better understanding of the request for support and to avoid errors, I would recommend that the work at the counter be done in pairs.

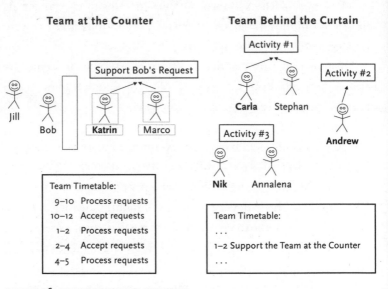

FIGURE 36: PRACTICE OF THE COUNTER

- Set a schedule determining when people needing support can freely access the counter and when the team at the counter can work on answering their requests. For instance, in the example shown in Figure 36, people in need of support can access the counter and request support from Katrin and Marco from 10:00 to 12:00 and from 2:00 to 4:00. Nobody can access the counter from 9:00 to 10:00, from 1:00 to 2:00, or from 4:00 to 5:00. In those time slots, Katrin and Marco will work to collect the information needed to process the requests.

- Set a schedule specifying when the team behind the curtain will support the team at the counter. In the example shown in Figure 36, the "team at work"— Carla, Stephan, Nik, Annalena, and Andrew—will work on supporting the team at the counter—Marco and Katrin. They will process the queue of requests for support that the team at the counter was not able to deal with.

☞ The schedules of the two teams should enable the team behind the curtain to consult the team at the counter if they need to clarify some aspects of the requests for support they received. In Figure 36, such collaboration can take place from 1:00 to 2:00.

- Set the frequency of the Pomodoro Rotations. As usual, the people responsible for the activities stay put and coworkers from the microteams in the team behind the curtain rotate with coworkers from the microteams in the team at the counter. The frequency of the Pomodoro Rotations between these two teams is usually every four or eight Pomodoros, or on a daily basis. The more interchangeable the team members are and the more experience they have with the practice of Pomodoro Rotations, the more frequently the rotations can occur.

When people come up to the counter to make requests, one of three scenarios is possible:

1. The team at the counter knows how to deal with the person's request and can immediately support them. In Figure 36, this happens from 10:00 to 12:00 and from 2:00 to 4:00.
2. The team at the counter knows how to deal with the person's request but needs some time to provide the answer. In this case, the team at the counter writes down the request, estimates the time and effort needed to deal with it, and schedules a time the person needing support will receive their response. In Figure 36, this happens from 9:00 to 10:00, 1:00 to 2:00, and 4:00 to 5:00.
3. The team at the counter is unable to make an estimate or does not know how to deal with the request. In this case, the team at the counter writes down the request for support and adds it to a queue of requests that the team behind the curtain will deal with during a scheduled time slot. In Figure 36, this is from 1:00 to 2:00.

☞ This practice can be misunderstood. I have often seen new people be hired by companies and assigned solely to managing the counter. This decision makes sense in that it puts team members back "behind the curtain," working continuously on that team's goals. However, the downside is that, more often than not, the team loses the useful experience gained by the team working at the counter in identifying opportunities to improve the process or the product. For this reason, I would recommend that the team at the counter be made up of at least one team member from behind the curtain.

PROS AND CONS

The advantages of the Practice of the Counter are:

- **WIN-WIN SOLUTIONS.** You keep your clients and colleagues happy while ensuring the rest of the team works to reach the defined goals without distractions and interruptions.
- **SHARING KNOW-HOW.** Solving problems and responding to real requests is one of the best ways to get to know the system or the product you are working on.
- **IDENTIFYING FLAWS IN THE PROCESS OR PRODUCT.** Exposure to colleagues' or clients' requests over time reveals opportunities to improve the team's process.

The only disadvantage of this practice is that the team behind the curtain might take longer to reach its goals. This is because we moved people from that team behind the curtain to the team at the counter.

☞ In my experience, the team behind the curtain often takes less time to reach its goals. The capacity lost when team members leave the team behind the curtain can be more than compensated for by the time saved managing interruptions. In other words, the time and effort needed to reach the goal with six people with no interruptions can be less than the time needed by eight people with interruptions.

THE PRACTICE OF
THE POMODORO HACKATHON

Whatever your age, if you enjoy challenges, I recommend you take part in a Hackathon one day. The term "Hackathon" was coined in the 1990s, a curious combination of "hack" and "marathon." The "hack" in Hackathon does not so much refer to hacking unauthorized access to data in a computer system as it does to finding a working solution to a problem by hammering away at it. The solutions you end up with might not be elegant from a design perspective, but they should be effective. Hackathons can last hours or days and are usually held on weekends. They always involve a challenge, such as inventing a groundbreaking video game, pushing the limits of technology to improve health and safety at work, or finding innovative ways to improve mobility in a city. You can take part as an individual or as part of a team (but it is obviously much more fun in a team). The best solution normally wins a prize. I am not sure if people use the Pomodoro Technique at Hackathons, but I named this practice after their passionate participants.

PROBLEM

A microteam struggles to complete one particular activity. It could be an activity requiring a great deal of research or an activity characterized by a high degree of complexity or uncertainty. If not completed on time, this activity can become a bottleneck that stops the rest of the team from moving forward.

SOLUTION

For unusual, complex, or risky activities, the Practice of the Pomodoro Hackathon enables the team to consider and choose from several solutions in the least amount of time possible.

To show how this practice can be applied, let us imagine you are the organizer of a Pomodoro Hackathon. These are the steps involved in setting up a Hackathon:

1. Invite all or some of the members of the team to participate in the Pomodoro Hackathon. One big room is usually the best environment for this kind of event.
2. Nominate the Jury. Usually the Jury is the microteam who is having trouble completing the critical activity. The members of that microteam could also participate in the Pomodoro Hackathon. At other times, the Jury is external to the team: customers, users, or managers. Sometimes the Jury is made up of the whole team.
3. Set a time box of a certain number of Pomodoros. Four Pomodoros is my usual choice and in my experience is normally enough to get useful solutions. In any case, the length of the Pomodoro Hackathon may vary: it depends on the complexity and the urgency of the problem to

solve. One Pomodoro should be considered the minimum. When you communicate the length of the time box set, you must make it clear that the final deadline for delivering the solution is binding. If you set four Pomodoros, then after four Pomodoros the Hackathon ends.

4. Ask the participants in the Hackathon to organize themselves into microteams and choose the person responsible for the activity. The decision about the size of the microteams depends on the type and complexity of the challenge. I am a big fan of microteams made up of two people. Pairs are small and effective. The interchangeability of team members is another factor that can influence the decision about the size of microteams. For instance, if the theme of the Hackathon is "Let's find a new layout for our blog posts," and if your team is characterized by a high degree of specialization, you might want to have teams made up of one business analyst, one graphic designer, and one copywriter. If specialization is not an issue in your team, then you have more freedom in forming microteams.

☞ I usually prefer to let the team members form microteams spontaneously, and I always favor the creation of "unusual" microteams: microteams made up of people who do not usually work together. I know It Is reassuring to work with someone we are used to working with, but breaking this habit can lead to surprisingly innovative results.

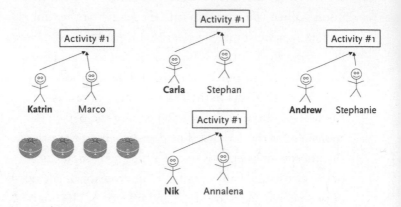

FIGURE 37: POMODORO HACKATHON—FOUR POMODOROS, FOUR MICRO-
TEAMS, ONE ACTIVITY

5. Give the same challenge—the activity you need a
   solution for—to the microteams participating in the
   Hackathon. All microteams will work on the same
   activity for the length of the time box you chose.
6. Wind up the timer for all the microteams participating in the Hackathon. For each Pomodoro, you will
   announce when the first 5 minutes have passed, when
   half a Pomodoro is over, and when there are only
   5 minutes remaining.

☞   Yes, I know, this is the first time I have used one timer for
    all the teams. In fact, this is the only situation in which
    I would recommend synchronizing the Pomodoro when
    working in a team. Why? Because I want to protect the

Pomodoro breaks in a context characterized by challenge, complexity, and urgency. People like challenges and, especially at their first Pomodoro Hackathon, might think that they can work through four Pomodoros or more with no breaks. Your role is to remind them of the purpose of the Pomodoro breaks. "The challenge is okay, but we don't want to feel exhausted after four Pomodoros! We want to feel in control and lucid during every Pomodoro." You want to help them. "Forcing" them to take real breaks in this kind of challenge is helpful.

7. Announce the winner. At the end of the time box you assigned for the Hackathon, the Jury assesses every microteam's solution, and selects the best one. I usually set one Pomodoro for the Jury to assess the solutions and one Pomodoro for them to show the winning solution to the participants. But my favorite scenario is the one where the Jury comprises all the Hackathon's participants. In this case, in the first Pomodoro, each microteam can quickly present their solution, and in the second Pomodoro the microteams assess and vote for the best solution. Why do I like this scenario? First, because all participants in the Hackathon can have a shared knowledge of the solution to be implemented, and second, because more often than not this is the moment when new ideas emerge that improve on the solution that was found.

Of course success is not guaranteed. What if no effective solution has been found in the time box you set for your Pomodoro Hackathon? This can happen. You can then simply organize another round. If this is the case, though, give the teams a longer break.

For the first round of the Hackathon, I would not recommend rotating coworkers between microteams. However, in any subsequent rounds, it is a good idea to swap members. In my experience, it is often the microteams that do not look like a good match on paper that end up producing the most creative results.

PROS AND CONS

The advantage of organizing a Pomodoro Hackathon is that teams can quickly generate many solutions to a critical activity. When your team feels stuck and needs an immediate, innovative solution to an often complex problem, being able to have and compare several solutions is incredibly valuable.

The disadvantage is that all the microteams involved in the Pomodoro Hackathon are unable to work on their current activities.

THE PRACTICE OF THE RAM

THE ASSYRIANS ARE credited with inventing the battering ram back in the eighth century B.C. I remember reading the description of this, the simplest war machine, by the Roman architect and writer Vitruvius in his work *On Architecture*. The battering ram was simple and destructive: a log with a bronze cap at its end shaped like a ram. In Roman times, almost no fortification could withstand it. If a copy of *On Architecture* should ever come your way, it is definitely worth a read.

Today, the "walls" we face are the seemingly impenetrable problems that prevent us from reaching our goals. Our battering ram is our ability to generate and apply a variety of solutions. Every new idea we test on the problem is like a blow of the ram hitting the wall. When you feel stuck in front of that wall, encountering another person's perspective increases the chances of coming up with a new idea. The more times we can repeat this process with new people, the more likely it is that the wall will be unable to withstand our blows and we will reach our goal.

PROBLEM

Let us imagine we have a team composed of four microteams of two people each. Each of the four pairs is working on a different activity. In each pair, one member is responsible for the activity (Figure 38).

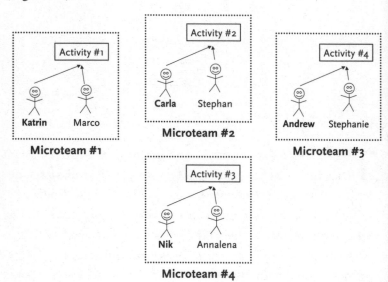

Activity #1
Katrin Marco
Microteam #1

Activity #2
Carla Stephan
Microteam #2

Activity #4
Andrew Stephanie
Microteam #3

Activity #3
Nik Annalena
Microteam #4

FIGURE 38: THE TEAM

Activity #1 has proved to be more complex than predicted. The microteam working on it is struggling and has no idea how to proceed. Completing this activity is essential if the whole team is to reach its goals. If not completed on time, this activity becomes a bottleneck for the other microteams (Figure 39).

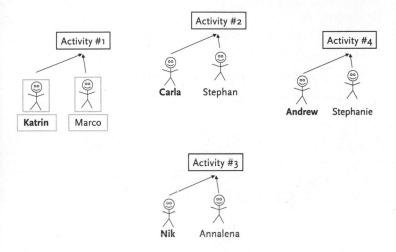

FIGURE 39: MICROTEAM #1 IS UNABLE TO COMPLETE ITS ACTIVITY

The other microteams are working hard to complete activities that are needed to reach the team's goals. Their work cannot be interrupted.

Microteam #1 has tried repeatedly, but unsuccessfully, to complete the activity. It seems necessary to find a way to apply the collective intelligence and problem solving abilities of the whole team to this problem.

SOLUTION

The Practice of the Ram enables teams to complete an activity by using the experience of all their members while maintaining their flow. Such a practice is particularly useful to complete activities on time in order to avoid creating bottlenecks for the rest of the team.

Here is how this practice can help Microteam #1 to complete their activity:

1. The person responsible for Microteam #1—the microteam in the grip of crisis—asks the rest of the team for help and briefly explains the problem.

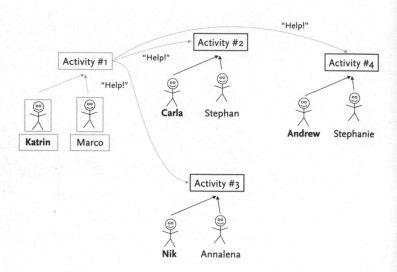

FIGURE 40: HELP!

2. For the other microteams, this is an external interruption (Figure 40). Now alerted to the critical situation, each person responsible for the other microteams agrees to swap his or her coworker with one of the coworkers on Microteam #1. Microteams #2 and #3 can swap from the next Pomodoro, whereas Microteam #4 prefers to swap after two Pomodoros.

3. Based on the complexity of the problem, and the availability of the different microteams, Katrin, the person responsible for Activity #1, quickly draws up a roster (Figure 41) with the names of the rotating coworkers: the members of the microteams who will work with her.

Practice of the Ram:
3-step, 3-Pomodoro Plan of Action

First Pomodoro: Swap Marco from Microteam #1 with Stephan from Microteam #2

Second Pomodoro: Swap Stephan from Microteam #1 with Annalena from Microteam #3

Third Pomodoro: Swap Annalena from Microteam #1 with Stephanie from Microteam #4

FIGURE 41: THE ROSTER

4. This roster is then shared with the other microteams. All the microteams will maintain the same number of people, two, but one person will be swapped in and out of Microteam #1. At each Pomodoro there will be a new coworker. **At each Pomodoro, the ram will hit harder and harder, battering down the problem that needs solving.**

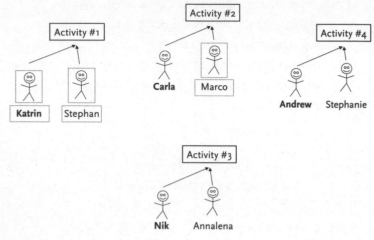

5. At the start of the new Pomodoro (Figure 42), the
   person responsible for the activity in Microteam #1
   continues to work on their task but with a different
   coworker until the end of the Pomodoro. In the first
   five minutes of the Pomodoro, Katrin from Microteam #1 explains the difficulty they are facing to the
   new coworker. In the final 5 minutes of the Pomodoro, Katrin will ask her coworker for feedback.

☞ The person responsible for Activities #2, #3, and #4
   goes through the same process of taking 5 minutes to
   get the new coworker up to speed and the last 5 minutes
   to get feedback from them.

If after the first Pomodoro the problem has still not been resolved, the person responsible for the activity remains and the next rotation shown in the roster takes place. Katrin continues working on Activity #1. Annalena replaces Stephan and starts working with Katrin. Stephan joins Nik working on Activity #3. Simply, the person responsible for the activity stays put and the other people rotate around.

☞ In microteams made up of more than two people, it is advisable to rotate no more than one person at a time.

In this example, Katrin drew up a roster based on three Pomodoros. What happens if this is not enough to solve the problem? If necessary, the person responsible for the activity can apply the Practice of the Ram again.

In the best scenario, the cry for help and the interruption it leads to is managed efficiently: The person responsible for the activity where the problem has arisen is able to explain the issue to the team members and, with their help, quickly come up with a roster. In this case, the Pomodoros under way in each microteam keep ticking. If the interruption has not been managed and the roster is not ready within 30 seconds, the people responsible for the activities must void their Pomodoros.

☞ Thirty seconds might seem too short to manage the process of explaining a problem and drawing up a roster. Practice makes it possible. Here are some simple guidelines to speed up the process: The person who asks for help only interrupts when they are sure they can describe the problem in one sentence. At a request for help, the other microteams immediately interrupt their work and focus on that request. The coworkers working in the other microteams who think they can help with the problem immediately convey their willingness to volunteer.

PROS AND CONS

The advantages of applying the Practice of the Ram are:

- The problem faced by one microteam—Microteam #1 in Figure 40—is shared with the team as a whole, and the person responsible for the related activity benefits from the skills and experience of different team members.
- The other microteams—Microteams #2, #3, and #4 in Figure 40—can continue working on their activities.
- The people in charge of those microteams can benefit from swapping coworkers, because this can lead to the sharing of knowledge.

The disadvantage of this practice is that it requires interrupting all the team members in the various microteams.

RESULTS

OBSERVATIONS

THE POMODORO TECHNIQUE has been applied successfully to various types of activities: organizing work and study habits, writing books, drafting technical reports, preparing presentations, and managing projects, meetings, events, conferences, and training courses.

Here are some observations that have emerged from the experience of people and teams that have applied the Pomodoro Technique.

LEARNING TIME

It takes no time at all to apply the Pomodoro Technique. Mastering the technique takes from 7 to 20 days of constant application. When it is used by pairs or teams, it's easier to implement the technique consistently.

> ☞ Experience shows that applying the technique in teams or organizing work in pairs results in a shorter learning time and more consistent results. In these cases, each pair works with its own Pomodoro.

THE LENGTH OF THE POMODORO

In terms of how long a Pomodoro lasts, two forces have to be kept in balance to maximize effectiveness:

- The Pomodoro has to represent an effective atomic measure of work. In other words, the Pomodoro has to measure equal units of continuous effort; in this form, these units are comparable with others. The problem is that, as everyone knows, all time is not equal in terms of the output of effort. All months aren't equal: December is shorter in terms of the number of productive days, and so is August in Mediterranean countries. Similarly, all the weeks in a month aren't equal: We don't make the same effort in every week. All the days in a week aren't equal: On some days you can work 8 hours, on others only 5 (especially if you need to go somewhere), and on still others you may work 10 to 12 hours (less often, I hope). Even all the hours in a day aren't equal: Not every hour produces the same amount of effort, mostly because of interruptions. As a unit of measure, much smaller time intervals such as 10 minutes may not be interrupted, but they don't allow us to achieve appreciable results, and tracking becomes too intrusive. Thus, as far as this first force is concerned, half an hour seems to be ideal.
- The Pomodoro has to encourage consciousness, concentration, and clear-minded thinking. It's been proved that 20- to 45-minute time intervals can max-

imize a person's attention and mental activity if they are followed by a short break.

In the light of these two forces, we've come to consider the ideal Pomodoro to be 20 to 35 minutes long, 40 minutes at the most. Experience shows that the Pomodoro Technique works best with 30-minute periods.

☞ In various work groups that experimented with the Pomodoro Technique in mentoring activities, each team was allowed to choose the length of its own Pomodoro on the condition that that choice be based on observations of effectiveness. Generally, the teams started off with hourlong Pomodoros (25 minutes seemed too short at first), then moved to 2 hours, then went down to 45 minutes, then to 10, till they finally settled on 30 minutes.

VARYING THE LENGTH OF BREAKS
The length of breaks depends on how tired you feel. Breaks at the end of a set should last from 15 to 30 minutes. For example, if you've kept up an intense rhythm throughout the day, at the end of the next to last set of Pomodoros your break will naturally last 25 minutes. If you have to solve a very complicated problem, you'll need a 25-minute break between the sets. If you're especially tired, it's possible and even beneficial to lengthen the breaks between sets every so often. But breaks that consistently exceed 30 minutes can interrupt the rhythm between sets of

Pomodoros. More important, this sets off an alarm signaling the need for rest and free time.

It would be a serious mistake to take shorter breaks between sets because you're under pressure. Your mind needs time to integrate old information and get ready to receive new information to solve the problems in the next Pomodoro. Taking a shorter break because you're in a rush could lead to a mental block in finding solutions.

☞ For beginners, once the last Pomodoro in the set of four is up, it's a good idea to set the timer for 25 minutes and start the break. The aim here isn't to impose 25 minutes rigidly but to ensure that you don't go over 30 minutes of break time. This should be done only at the beginning. In time, you'll realize how tired you are and understand when you're refreshed and ready to start again.

The same can be said for breaks between Pomodoros, which should be no less than 3 to 5 minutes. When you're especially tired, you can stop working for up to 10 minutes. Remember, though, that downtime between Pomodoros that consistently lasts more than 5 to 10 minutes can break the rhythm between Pomodoros. It would be better to finish the current set and take a 15- to 30-minute break. The best way to manage your resources is to work strategically, first by increasing the breaks between sets and then by extending the breaks between Pomodoros if necessary.

The most fitting metaphor for managing breaks is long-distance runners. At the start of the marathon, they know they have the energy to run faster, but they also know their limits and the difficulty of the challenge ahead. They manage their resources to achieve the best result at the finish line.

A DIFFERENT PERCEPTION OF TIME

The first benefit that comes from applying the Pomodoro Technique, which is apparent in the first few days, is the sharper focus and concentration that comes from a different perception of time. This new perception of passing time seems to elicit the following sensations:

1. The first 25-minute Pomodoros seem to pass more slowly.
2. After a few days of constant application of the Pomodoro, users say they can feel the midway point of the 25 minutes.
3. By the end of the first week of constant application of the Pomodoro, users say they can feel when 5 minutes are left on the Pomodoro. In fact, many people report having a sense of fatigue during those final minutes.

We can stimulate the ability to feel time in a different way by means of a series of exercises that enhance consciousness of passing time among Pomodoro users. This different awareness of the passage of time seems to lead Pomodoro users to a higher level of concentration in performing the activity at hand.

SOUNDS OF THE POMODORO

The Pomodoro emits two sounds: It ticks, and it rings (after 25 minutes). In regard to these sounds, there are several things to consider from two different perspectives: Pomodoro users and people sharing the same work space with Pomodoro users.

PEOPLE WHO USE THE POMODORO

When Pomodoro users start applying the Pomodoro Technique, the ticking and ringing can be annoying. There are various ways to make these sounds softer, but experience shows that in time (even with just a few days of constant application) two things happen:

- The ticking becomes a calming sound. "It's ticking, and I'm working and everything's fine."
- After a while, users don't even hear the ring because their level of concentration is so high. In fact, not hearing the Pomodoro ring becomes a real problem in some cases.

Clearly, the different sensations that are elicited by the same sounds are signs of a profound change in a person's perception of passing time.

PEOPLE WHO ARE SUBJECT TO THE POMODORO

Now consider people who have to "put up with" the Pomodoro. This situation may arise when the technique is used in a shared space; for example, study halls at a university or an open-space work environment.

To respect the people who don't use the Pomodoro, a number of solutions have been tested. In order of effectiveness, these are: watches that count down 25 minutes and then flash or beep softly, cell phones with software applications that vibrate or make the display flash, and kitchen timers with muted rings.

The ticking and ringing of several Pomodoros in an environment where a team is using the Pomodoro Technique isn't considered bothersome.

SHAPES OF THE POMODORO

Obviously, the kitchen timer you use doesn't have to be shaped like a tomato. Apples, pears, oranges, toasters, cooks, spheres, UFOs—the market for timers is as varied as it is upbeat. Choosing your own Pomodoro (we should say "timer") makes the technique more enjoyable and accessible.

RING ANXIETY

When one is learning the technique, there may be some anxiety during the first few Pomodoros from the feeling of being controlled by the Pomodoro. Experience shows that this feeling emerges most frequently in two cases:

- Among people who are not used to self-discipline
- Among people who are very oriented toward achieving results

In both cases, it will prove difficult to concentrate on the primary objective of the technique: empowering each person to improve his or her work or study process through self-observation.

For people who aren't used to self-discipline, ring anxiety

generally arises from the fear that the Pomodoro Technique might be used to monitor their progress externally. It's important to stress that the aim of the technique is not to carry out any sort of external analysis or control. With the Pomodoro Technique, there is no inspector who monitors workers' hours and methods in an oppressive fashion. The Pomodoro Technique must not be misconstrued as a form of this kind of external control. Instead, the technique was created to satisfy the personal need to improve, and it has to be applied spontaneously.

Cases of results-oriented people are more common. If every tick seems like an invitation to work quickly and if every tock repeats the question "Am I going fast enough?" these are signs of full immersion in what we might call the *Becoming* Syndrome. Today this is quite common. The underlying fear people have here is usually the inability to demonstrate their effectiveness as fully as they'd like to others and to themselves. The Pomodoro is a method for comparison, if not with others then at least with themselves, and every tick and tock seems to reveal their lack of ability. Under pressure from time that passes, they look for shortcuts, but this isn't the way to go faster; shortcuts lead to defects and interruptions that feed into their fear of time in a vicious circle. How can they hear the ticking as a calming sound? The idea or the solution might be just around the corner with the next tick, but they'll miss it if they keep thinking about how quickly time is passing.

The first thing to learn with the Pomodoro Technique is that seeming fast isn't important; reaching the point of actually being fast is. You do this by learning to measure yourself, observe how you work, and develop the value of continuity. This is why the first objective to achieve with the Pomodoro Technique is simply to mark down the Pomodoros you've completed.

If it takes four Pomodoros to draft a simple two-page review, it's not important that you expected to finish in two Pomodoros or that you want to show everyone that you can finish in two. What's important is to find out how to go from four to two.

The initial challenge is knowing how to analyze the way you work on the basis of test measurements collected every 30 minutes and not having expectations about the result. Simply work, track, observe, and change to improve if you need to. Once this is understood, the ticking starts to have a different sound. You need to concentrate to be fast.

The next step is to estimate and—why not?—even challenge yourself to succeed in completing a particular activity within the estimated time. This is one of the rules of the game for the Pomodoro Technique, but never take shortcuts! The Xs marking completed Pomodoros are frustrating when they get closer and closer to the last estimated Pomodoro box. But you have to be brave and keep on working, staying calm and concentrating, to be successful. Stimulating the value of continuity leads to productivity and creativity. Every tick of the Pomodoro, if you hear it, is an invitation to stay focused and alert and to continue.

☞ At first, even getting through a single Pomodoro a day without interruptions is an excellent result, because it allows you to observe your process. The next day your effort will be focused on completing at least one Pomodoro with no interruptions, possibly two or more. With the Pomodoro Technique, the number of Pomodoros you finish doesn't matter so much as the pathway to consistently achieving more Pomodoros. This same incremental approach should be used when you take up the Pomodoro Technique again after you haven't used it for a while (for example, when you get back from a vacation). In this case, it takes patience and a bit of training to reach 10 to 12 Pomodoros a day consistently.

CONSTANT INTERNAL INTERRUPTIONS

When you perceive internal interruptions as things that can't be postponed, it becomes difficult to complete even a single Pomodoro in a whole day. In these cases, we suggest that you set the Pomodoro for 25 minutes and force yourself, Pomodoro after Pomodoro, to increase (and, more important, never reduce) the time you work nonstop. The final objective is to get to the 25-minute mark having worked continuously, with no interruptions: "In this Pomodoro I've managed to work for ten minutes without interruptions; in the next one I'm going to work no less than ten minutes, maybe even just one minute more." Results come Pomodoro after Pomodoro.

THE NEXT POMODORO WILL GO BETTER

The feeling of having time to do things and not using it well is often incapacitating. Your mind starts wandering from the past to the future: "If only I'd done that research on the Internet yesterday, and if only I'd sent that e-mail last week. How am I going to deliver the report by next week?" This provokes feelings of guilt and creates anxiety-filled situations.

The Pomodoro Technique allows you to keep your focus on the current Pomodoro or, once that's done, the next Pomodoro. Your attention is on the here and now, emphasizing the search for a concrete way to stimulate the value of continuity and carry out activities in the most reasonable order.

When you feel lost, a Pomodoro can be dedicated to exploration to get your priorities straight and lay out a new plan. If your ideas are clear but something's missing—maybe determination, maybe a bit of courage—don't sit around waiting. Wind up the Pomodoro and start working.

People who have the habit of procrastinating say that they benefit from the fact that the Pomodoro enables them to concentrate and achieve little things (activities that take five to seven Pomodoros' worth of effort at the most), without having to worry about everything. One Pomodoro at a time, one activity at a time, one objective at a time. For personality types with a strong tendency to procrastinate, it's important to realize that the initial objective is to finish one Pomodoro—25 minutes of work on a particular activity—without interruptions.

WHAT TYPE OF TIMER WORKS BEST?

What kind of Pomodoro is most effective: a mechanical timer or a piece of software? Speaking from experience, the most effective Pomodoro is always the kitchen timer. In any case, to guarantee the greatest possible effectiveness, the Pomodoro has to meet a number of requirements:

- You have to be able to wind it up. The act of winding up the Pomodoro is a declaration of your determination to start working on the activity at hand.
- It has to show clearly how much time is left, and it should make a ticking sound as time passes. This is a way to practice feeling time and stay focused.
- It should make an audible, easily identified sound to signal that time's up.

What's more, to mark the end of a Pomodoro or to eliminate a finished activity from the To Do Today Sheet, Pomodoro practitioners should use explicit gestures. For this reason, it's better if those gestures aren't automated.

IMPROVING ESTIMATES

One of the more tangible results that can be attained with the Pomodoro Technique involves improving the ability to estimate. This develops along two pathways:

- **IMPROVEMENT OF QUANTITATIVE ESTIMATES** by reducing the error between estimated Pomodoros and actual Pomodoros. In other words, when one is planning the day's tasks, the effort needed to complete a specific activity can be predicted accurately. Self-observation and 30-minute measurements are the basis for more exact estimates. Experience shows that a positive sign of improvement in estimation occurs when the number of cases of underestimation is equal to the number of cases of overestimation. A strategy oriented toward systematic overestimation or underestimation does not lead to quantitative improvement. Learning to estimate is essential to being effective.

- **IMPROVEMENT OF QUALITATIVE ESTIMATES** by reducing the number of activities that were not included in the planning phase. In other words, while one is planning the day's tasks, the numbers and types of activities that actually have to be done can be pinpointed (weak version) or, even better, the specific set of activities that serve to achieve the given objective with the least possible effort can be identified (strong version). Overall underestimation happens when we don't correctly identify the activities that have to be done or don't realize that the activities we have identified aren't the most effective. With the Pomodoro Technique, unplanned activities are tracked when they emerge. Observing and understanding the nature of these activities allows Pomodoro users to hone their forecasting and organizing skills.

Why does the Pomodoro Technique improve both aspects of estimation? One of the common causes of quantitative and qualitative improvement is that the activities we measure are continually divided up according to the following rule: **If it takes more than five to seven Pomodoros, break it down**.

Smaller activities are more understandable and easier to estimate, and so the margin of error shrinks. Smaller activities (but not too small) enable us to recognize simpler solutions. In fact, the aim of breaking down activities should never be simply to divide them up as far as possible. Instead, the point is to identify incremental paths that have the least possible complexity.

MOTIVATION AND THE POMODORO

With the Pomodoro Technique, three factors contribute to boosting personal motivation:

- Completing several activities a day that aren't too simple or too complex **(Rule: If it takes more than five to seven Pomodoros, break it down)** and that help you reach your objective
- Directly influencing personal improvement on a day-to-day basis
- Being aware of how you work/how you're working thanks to continual observation and measurement

AND IF EVERYTHING GOES COMPLETELY WRONG?

What should you do if you get caught up in a rush or have a case of nerves or a panic attack? If you start feeling the anxiety of *becoming* and the deadline is getting closer by the second? What should you do in the case of total paralysis? That can happen. It's only human. The Pomodoro Technique is extremely useful in these circumstances.

First, take a look at the situation. Try to understand what went wrong during the last Pomodoro. If necessary, reorganize activities; be open to new things to include and innovative strategies for pinpointing essential tasks. Focus on the next Pomodoro. Keep on working. Concentration and consciousness lead to speed, one Pomodoro at a time.

If you're especially tired, you need to organize shorter sets (e.g., three Pomodoros) and take longer breaks between sets. The more tired you are or the more behind or panic-stricken you feel, the more important it is to repeat and review rather than forge ahead at all costs. The key objective is never to recover lost time but instead to be focused on taking the next step on your chosen path, which you often—consciously—change.

THE POMODORO HAS A LIMIT

The main disadvantage of the Pomodoro Technique is that to reach your goals effectively, you need to accept help from a little mechanical object. Discontinuing the use of the Pomodoro Technique actually diminishes most of the positive effects described above. Though you retain the ability to break down activities incrementally and may keep taking short breaks, the discipline ensured by the Pomodoro seems to be the key to maintaining a high level of effectiveness.

WHEN NOT TO USE THE POMODORO

The Pomodoro Technique shouldn't be used for activities you do in your free time. In fact, use of the Pomodoro would make these activities scheduled and goal-oriented. That's no longer free time. If you decide to read a book simply for pleasure, you shouldn't use the Pomodoro Technique. This is unscheduled free time.

MASTERING THE TECHNIQUE

I N ACTUAL FACT, the positive effects of the Pomodoro Technique on individual or team productivity come from a number of different factors. Those factors are summarized below.

INVERTING THE DEPENDENCY ON TIME

The Pomodoro represents an abstraction of time, a box that can hold and limit *becoming* and on which time depends in the end. It's precisely by breaking and inverting our dependency on *becoming* that a different vision of time emerges. By measuring ourselves against a finite abstraction of time—the Pomodoro—we can succeed in breaking our direct dependency on the concept of *becoming*.

Specifically, the time-boxing concept and the typical Pomodorian notion of time running backward (from 25 minutes to 0) generate positive tension (*eustress*) that can facilitate the decision-making process. In general terms, this stimulates the vital contact you need to assert yourself and at the same time accomplish activities.

The passage of time is perceived no longer as negative but as positive. Every Pomodoro represents the opportunity to improve or, in crisis situations, to reorganize rapidly. The more time passes, the better the chance to improve your process. The more time passes, the more easily activities can be estimated and scheduled. The more time passes, the more the feeling of anxiety is assuaged, and in its place come enhanced consciousness, sharper focus on the here and now, and a clearer mind in deciding on your next move. The result is higher productivity.

Moreover, the same dependency inversion mechanism is applied in the Pomodoro Technique to reduce and eliminate interruptions. This increases concentration and continuity in work, and here, too, there is a considerable correlated rise in productivity.

REGULATING COMPLEXITY

We can maximize our motivation by accomplishing several challenging activities every day that are neither too complex nor too easy simply by applying the following rules:

- **If it takes more than five to seven Pomodoros, break it down.**
- **If it takes less than one Pomodoro, add it up.**

Less complex activities are usually easier to estimate, and so quantitative estimates improve. Breaking down activities so that they deliver incremental value also bolsters our determination to attain our objectives.

DETACHMENT

Frequent breaks with the Pomodoro are essential to achieving more lucid, conscious, and effective mental capacity with a resulting increase in productivity. It is important to note that in many environments there is an aversion to breaks, as if they were a sign of weakness. Common wisdom in many companies seems to be "Real managers start the meeting at 9 a.m. and end at 10 p.m. and never leave their office." This extreme behavior at work often lays a solid foundation for frustration, poor concentration, and, consequently, ineffectiveness.

By applying the Pomodoro Technique, many people have begun to understand the value and effectiveness of detachment. A break every 25 minutes lets you see things from a different perspective and enables you to come up with different solutions; you often find mistakes to correct, and your creative processes are stimulated. Detachment enhances the value of continuity.

But the break really has to be a break. It does not consist simply of stopping an activity when the 25-minute buzzer rings or when a set is finished and continuing to think about that task during the break. With the Pomodoro Technique, you get used to stopping and disengaging from continuous work situations that don't improve individual or team effectiveness. Stopping, detaching, and observing yourself from the outside enhance awareness of your behavior. Stopping becomes synonymous with strength, not weakness.

OBSERVATION AND CONTINUAL FEEDBACK

The Pomodoro Technique represents a method of comparison every 25 minutes. The first and last 5 minutes of a Pomodoro, which serve to review and repeat what you've done, enable you to realize whether a certain course of action is effective. Pair work magnifies this positive phenomenon more than does individual or group work. In the most critical cases, it's possible to change direction from the very next Pomodoro, rescheduling the activities that need to be done.

Recording data at least once a day, with tracking every 30 minutes, lets us assess the effectiveness of our modus operandi on the basis of objective metrics. By observing what you've recorded, you can make a decision to modify your process, improving the content of activities, defining clearer objectives or breaking down activities, identifying and eliminating duplicated or unnecessary activity or phases, and testing alternative strategies for assembling activities while reducing error in qualitative estimates.

The chance to affect your work or study process directly by steering it toward improvement stimulates your personal interest in accomplishing activities by asserting yourself.

SUSTAINABLE PACE

Respecting the timetable for work and breaks contributes to the achievement of continuity. In fact, to guarantee consistently high productivity, it is not effective to make yourself work or study nonstop from morning till night. An industrial machine certainly produces more if it works a long time without stopping, but human beings don't function like industrial machines.

By respecting the schedule for breaks between single Pomodoros and sets of Pomodoros, you can work and study while maintaining your pace. You'll get tired, which is only natural, but you won't become exhausted. In other words, by consciously managing breaks and the complexity of content, in time, anyone who uses the Pomodoro Technique can come to know his or her sustainable pace or physiological rhythm.

THE NEXT STEP

Ready to go? Already have a timer? Downloaded the templates and worksheets from the Pomodoro Technique website? Then let's get started.

A path of improvement lies before you that involves discipline, observation, and fun. Setting the timer and working with the Pomodoro Technique will provide you with positive results even before you have reached the first of the technique's six objectives.

What could help you take the next step? Here are a few tips and suggestions to keep you on the path of step-by-step improvement:

- **EACH AND EVERY POMODORO IS IMPORTANT.** The objective of the entire technique is to develop personal awareness of time; that is, to become aware of each of your next steps. With each step, you support the development of this awareness. Observation requires effort and discipline, and so you need to collect information about how you work—and you need to do it in a systematic way. It's great to amaze ourselves with our improvements and to rid ourselves of illusions along the way.

- **YOU DON'T HAVE TO COMPETE WITH TIME.** With the Pomodoro Technique, time is a tool that promotes your work if it is used in a conscious way. Awareness is the objective, and time is the tool. Would you compete with a hammer? There's no point. In some cases, you may feel the desire to prevail over time; for example, when you feel the need to complete a high number of Pomodoros by the end of the day to beat some record. In doing so, however, you already have lost, for as Baudelaire said: "Time is a greedy player who wins without cheating, every round."[1] Any form of competition with time is destined to fail. Suppose that during one of these competitions you suddenly realize what you are doing. Then what? What should you do? Stop the Pomodoro and take a deep breath. Remember: **The next Pomodoro will go better.**

- **TAKE BREAKS.** The break is the most important structural element of the Pomodoro Technique. Breaks allow you to step away for a moment, recognize fatigue, and decide whether to stop or continue. By taking a break you will begin the next Pomodoro with greater clarity and willingness to work. Breaks make us more productive, and they don't involve any work.

---

[1] Charles Baudelaire, *Flowers of Evil*, Oxford University Press, 2008.

- **ACHIEVE ONE OBJECTIVE AT A TIME.** The Pomodoro Technique is divided into a series of incremental objectives. Success in reaching each objective is fostered by conscious application and success with previous objectives. To determine whether you have truly achieved an objective and to avoid deceiving yourself, it can be useful to formulate the expected improvements that should be obtained from the various objectives by asking questions to which you can answer yes or no:

  - Have I been more alert and clearheaded using the first and last few minutes of the Pomodoro to review what I have done?
  - Have I found that revising and repeating activities is more effective if it is done aloud?
  - Have I found that revising and repeating activities is more effective when it is done with a partner?

If you notice that you keep answering no and cannot easily achieve a certain objective, ask yourself if you have applied the previous objectives fully and consciously. In any case, hold off on working on an objective until you have achieved the previous ones.

- **THERE IS NO NEED TO RUSH.** Your objective is not to reach all the objectives of the Pomodoro Technique in as little time as possible; that would just be another way of competing with time. Yes, slow down. There's no reason to rush. Take your time. Enjoy the way in which you achieve the current objective. Pleasure does not come from hurrying on nervously to the next objective but from consciously experiencing the current one.

Enough said. Now it's Pomodoro Time. Let the fun begin!

RULES

A Pomodoro consists of 25 minutes plus a 5-minute break *(p. 30)*.

After every four Pomodoros, take a 15- to 30-minute break *(p. 33)*.

The Pomodoro is indivisible.
There are no half or quarter Pomodoros *(pp. 31, 49, 53)*.

If a Pomodoro begins, it has to ring *(p. 35)*.

If a Pomodoro is interrupted definitively, it's void *(p. 31)*.

If you complete an activity during a Pomodoro, review your work until the Pomodoro rings *(p. 35)*.

Protect the Pomodoro.
Inform effectively, negotiate quickly to reschedule the interruption, and get back to the person who interrupted you, as agreed *(p. 51)*.

If it takes more than five to seven Pomodoros, break it down.
Complex activities should be divided into several activities *(pp. 58, 64, 137, 138, 141)*.

If it takes less than one Pomodoro, add it up.
Simple tasks can be combined *(pp. 58, 60, 141)*.

Results are achieved Pomodoro after Pomodoro *(p. 134)*.

The Timetable Always Overrides the Pomodoro *(pp. 72, 91)*.

One Microteam, One Pomodoro.
Each microteam has and manages its own Pomodoro *(pp. 88, 90)*.

The next Pomodoro will go better *(pp. 49, 53, 134, 145)*.

GLOSSARY

POMODORO. A kitchen timer used to measure 25-minute intervals. The name of the technique comes from the first timer used, which was shaped like a tomato (*pomodoro* in Italian).

TIME-BOXING. With this technique, once a series of activities has been assigned to a specific time interval, the delivery date for those activities should never change. If necessary, the unfinished activities can be reassigned to the next time interval.

QUALITATIVE ESTIMATION ERROR. This error occurs when all the activities needed to reach a certain goal have not been identified.

QUANTITATIVE ESTIMATION ERROR. This error occurs when the estimation of a single activity (or set of activities) is higher (over-estimation) or lower (underestimation) than the actual effort.

GET TO WORK

THE OFFICIAL WEBSITE
FrancescoCirillo.com/pages/pomodoro-technique

THE OFFICIAL BOOK SITE
FrancescoCirillo.com/products/the-pomodoro-technique

THE PUBLIC COURSE
FrancescoCirillo.com/products/pomodoro-technique-public-course

Learn directly from Francesco Cirillo, creator of the Pomodoro Technique, with this hands-on training course.

THE ONLINE COURSE
FrancescoCirillo.com/products/pomodoro-technique-online-course

Learn directly from Francesco Cirillo, creator of the Pomodoro Technique, with this online course.

CERTIFICATION

FrancescoCirillo.com/products/
certified-pomodoro-technique-practitioner

Become a Certified Pomodoro Technique Practitioner with this self-guided certification program that you can do from anywhere.

EVENTS AND MEETUPS

FrancescoCirillo.com/pages/calendar

Conferences and fun get-togethers where you can meet other Pomodoro Technique users, Francesco Cirillo, and members of the Pomodoro Team.

FACEBOOK

Facebook.com/francescocirilloconsulting

TWITTER

Twitter.com/pomodorotech

E-MAIL

pomodorotechnique@francescocirillo.com

TO DO TODAY

Name: _____

Date: _____

	UNPLANNED & URGENT	

ACTIVITY INVENTORY

Name: _____

RECORDS

Name: _____

DATE	TIME	TYPE	ACTIVITY	ESTIMATE	REAL	DIFF.

BIBLIOGRAPHY

Charles Baudelaire, *Flowers of Evil* (Oxford University Press, 2008),
    ISBN 978-0199535583.

Henri Bergson, *Creative Evolution* (Book Jungle, 2009),
    ISBN 978-1438528175.

Jerome Bruner, *The Process of Education* (Harvard University Press,
    1977), ISBN 978-0674710016.

Jane B. Burka and Lenora M. Yuen, *Procrastination: Why You Do It,
    What to Do About It Now* (Da Capo Lifelong Books, 2008),
    ISBN 978-0738211701.

Tony Buzan, *The Brain User's Guide* (Plume, 1983),
    ISBN 978-0525480457.

Hans-Georg Gadamer, *Truth and Method* (Continuum, 2004),
    ISBN 978-0826405852.

Tom Gilb, *Principles of Software Engineering Management* (Addison-
    Wesley, 1996), ISBN 978-0201192469.

Abraham H. Maslow, *Toward a Psychology of Being* (Wiley, 1998),
    ISBN 978-0471293095.

Eugène Minkowski, *Lived Time* (Northwestern University Press, 1970),
    ISBN 978-0810103221.

ACKNOWLEDGMENTS

FIRST AND FOREMOST, I want to thank my friend and mentor Giovanni Caputo, for having accompanied me yet again on this adventure.

Thanks also go to everyone who encouraged me to write and improve this book: Katrin Rampf, Marco Isella, Crawford McCubbin, Katharina Martina, Carlo Garatti, Lucy Vauclair, Michelle Ogata, Mick McGovern, Piergiuliano Bossi, Claudia Sandu, Meihua Su, Daniela Faggion, and Alessandra Del Vecchio, to name a few.

Thanks to all those who learned the Pomodoro Technique through my workshops; their feedback enabled me to observe the technique and improve it. In particular: Ann Wilson, Lee Sullivan, Katie Geddes, Simone Genini, Bruno Bossola, Giannandrea Castaldi, Roberto Crivelli, Ernesto Di Blasio, Alberto Quario, Loris Ugolini, Alberico Gualfetti, Marco Dani, Luigi Mengoni, Leonardo Marinangeli, Federico De Felici, and Nicola Canalini.

ABOUT THE AUTHOR

FRANCESCO CIRILLO is the inventor of the Pomodoro Technique. An innovator in process-improvement methods, as well as an entrepreneur, software designer, mentor, and instructor, Francesco has trained thousands of people around the world. He currently teaches at the Berlin School of Economics and Law. Francesco also runs Cirillo Consulting, where he develops new tools and techniques to improve individual and team productivity.

To learn more about
Francesco and Cirillo Consulting visit
www.FrancescoCirillo.com.